ENDURANCE
Going The Distance From The Valley To The Mountaintop

By Tricia Andreassen

Co-Authored by:
Desiree Anderson
Kate Bancroft
Wendell Betts
Jeanette Brewer
Jacquie Fazekas
Alyssa Harrington
B. Jacqueline Jeter
Tiffany Johnson
Dennis LaRue Jr.
Ruth Meed
Edward Reed
Carlos Vargas
Terry Wood

Creative Life
Publishing & Learning
INSTITUTE

Creative Life Publishing & Learning Institute
www.CLPLI.com
Info@CLPLI.com

Book Versions
Paperback ISBN: 978-1-946265-10-4
eBook ISBN: 978-1-946265-11-1
Amazon ISBN: 978-1-946265-12-8

Cover Design By Dara Rogers

CONTENTS

FOREWORD

Throughout all the years of my life, I have seen many things, heard many stories, experienced many challenges. I have not catalogued or organized them. I have not measured their impact on my life. Then I met Tricia Andreassen.

Our conversations have taken me on a journey of the heart to consider the impact others have had on my life in a way I had not considered before. So that I now can truly say, when Tricia my new sister in Christ speaks, I listen!

Has the word *ENDURANCE* been a major word in your conversations? Not in mine! Now I realize why: I've never really documented the sequences and consequences of my lengthy life as situations and incidences of *ENDURANCE*. I had not mined the insights waiting there. I had not benefited as I could from seeing the wisdom in common threads of interaction in the tapestry.

Reading this series of powerful true stories has opened my eyes to the majesty of love which God has shown to us by the incidences in our lives that reveal the strength of our personal *ENDURANCE*. See for yourself *the power you have to thrive*, when it seems that all around you is failing!

- Dr. Thelma Wells
D.D., Founder *A Woman of God Ministries and Generation Love Conferences*, Professor, Speaker, Author, Mentor

THE ULTIMATE STORY OF ENDURANCE

By Tricia Andreassen

THE ULTIMATE STORY OF ENDURANCE

As I sit here in my prayer room, I process all the stories and the private conversations I have spent with each of these incredible people that God has brought forward to share their message of ENDURANCE.

Honestly, I don't even know where to start as the unfolding journey of this book has in itself been so filled with miracles and divine connection that just the melding of these people coming together are a story within itself. You see, just a few days ago, God laid it on my heart to go back to all the writings that had been done up to this point. He directed me that, just by looking at them with a higher level of awareness, these writings would reveal that all He had foretold about the coming together of our growing community is actually happening right now in the Unstoppable Warriors movement—that includes the fact that even that a person like you would be reading this book at this moment!

As I looked through my writings from 2015 to present day, God also directed me to pull all of my journals that I had written in specifically since 2005. It was in the gathering and reading of these writings and in the watching of videos I had made here and there (not as consistently as I do today) that I realized how He had been calling me in each and every decade of my life.

Just in the last 48 hours, I realized I had been telling folks about the big shift that had happened in my life in August of 2014 which brought me to where I am today. Simultaneously, I realized that God has been beside me all along guiding me, knocking on my heart, and continuously prodding me before that shift in 2014 for what He believed in me. Here, GOD WAS GOING THE DISTANCE—forever enduring in His patience with me to step fully into my life and ministry purpose to serve Him completely. Through this realization, my eyes were opened to an understanding I had never experience before.

It was July 18, 2017 when God revealed why the word ENDURANCE was so powerful and why He had awakened me with this word through a dream so real that I had to shake myself out of it and still have ENDURANCE on my mind.

Kate Bancroft, a co-author in this book as well as in *Stepping Into Courage*, flew down from Michigan to my North Carolina home to visit me. I had invited her to come so that we could just be together and let God lead our hearts to what He wanted to reveal to us and to how He might direct our future in working together. When Kate and I started connecting deeper in friendship, God revealed how closely and carefully He has yoked us to minister to those battling internal issues of self-worth, self-image, betrayal, depression, eating disorders, grief and loss. We realized that we have a God-appointed relationship—even though we already strongly sensed this, it was overwhelmingly revealed that day.

The first morning when I awoke, I knew we were to go to a truly beautiful place an hour from our home called Moravian Falls, and afterwards to a very special place called Prayer Mountain. The night before, I battled things in my mind so disturbing it became clear to me that the enemy was doing whatever possible to cause a feeling of unworthiness within me. I had shared so much with Kate about painful chapters in my life that had involved business loss, friendship loss, burn-out and depression during that season. She had listened so openly and yet, when I had gone to bed, the enemy attacked through my insecurities saying that Kate would not like me anymore and she would see me as a flawed weak broken person. The enemy said I couldn't be friends with anyone like Kate because I was bad and once people knew the *"real me"* they would abandon me. With these thoughts swirling in my mind, I fell asleep continuing to battle these emotions and stories in my dreams, then waking up only to battle getting back to sleep.

The next morning, I got up around 5AM and my whole spirit just wanted to shed tears. I sat down to write out parts of the dream I could still recall. As I was writing, tears flowed down my cheeks in moments of quiet. The enemy was telling me that everything I had shared was bad, that I needed to *"shut up,"* and not share anymore about myself. I was even told by the enemy that Kate was probably calling the airline to leave early because she knew that she didn't want to be my friend anymore.

Shortly after my waking and writing in quiet, Kate emerged from her room saying *"Good morning!"* I didn't say much, then proceeded back to the front porch to process AND to lock the feelings away. Thankfully, I was praying, seeking God for understanding to my dream, and asking Him to help me. While Kate proceeded to come out on the front porch with her journal and Bible, God's voice rose over the enemy that had been chattering at me—and I began to share with her. I found the courage (Yes, oh yes Courage! This is why God had the book *Stepping Into Courage* come before this one) to ask Kate if I could read her my dream and she said, *"Yes"*. I bravely and vulnerably shared the dream that I had documented in my journal just hours before. I will never forget the look on her face when she said, *"Wow! You could have inserted my name into that journal entry and it would have been like it was my own journal entry."* She went on to share that she had also had fitful dreams, that the enemy had also attacked her mind saying that I wouldn't like her anymore, and that I would feel that it was a mistake having her come visit.

When I heard these things, my jaw about dropped to the ground! Here, I had been thinking that I was unworthy. The enemy had said that I was broken and couldn't have close women relationships because I was damaged goods, and here was Kate going through her own battle! Thank the Lord above that Kate and I both had the courage to open our hearts because, when we did, our Heavenly Father began to show us that our friendship was strong for His purposes and the enemy was trying to do everything possible to shut down the connection He had orchestrated.

After this realization and open conversation, we knew that God was with us and He would reveal so much more to us over the days we were to spend together. His promise was solidified as we drove on our trip to Moravian Falls celebrating! We arrived at the falls with our picnic in hand to enjoy along with our Bibles and Journals. While sitting there, we basked in the beauty of a 35 foot high waterfall and in the sound of its mighty rushing water. I began to share with Kate the history of the Moravians and how they had gathered together for many years to pray and worship together on this mountain. We continued to read about how their 24 hour prayer vigils led to the Spirit of the Lord blessing their ministry, and how the ministry spread God's Word all over the world to over 160 nations. After lunch, we walked over to the campground to see the owner of the land where the fall was located and to get the hand drawn map to Prayer Mountain. Anita, the owner, instantly connected with us as we shared our love for the Lord and our heart for conducting specific women retreats. My husband Kurt and I had visited the falls for the first time one or two years prior and I had remembered that they were building some homes by the falls that could be rented out. Anita continued to share that they had also purchased a larger home near their property which had a trail to the falls and she would give us a tour of all the properties.

During our time with Anita, God began to work and reveal signs of why our Unstoppable Warrior community was growing and how we were to be coming together for teaching, mentoring, learning and sharing God's Word all over the world like the Moravians had done. Looking back, I knew things were miraculously developing, but nowhere near what I feel in my veins at this moment of my fingers gliding over this keyboard. So much was being revealed: some was shown more completely and some was coming in pieces without complete clarity.

Anita pointed out mineral stripes that were in the shape of a sword running through a huge rock and immediately God reminded me of a vision of a woman warrior who was to go on a journey. I won't go into all of this vision now because this is a vision which has a full story of its own associated with it. At the top of the mountain where the lodge was situated to hold larger events, I saw a tree in the distance that was shown to me in the same vision of this warrior. I found it difficult to speak words as my mind moved from thought to thought to thought. The Spirit of God was so strong with us that, before pulling out of the driveway to head to Prayer Mountain, we joined hands sitting in my white Yukon to pray right then. I said to Kate, *"I just don't know what to say or how to process."* She replied, *"Just let it come! God will reveal more! Let's head to Prayer Mountain!"*

The campground owner Anita had mentioned to us that an intense storm had come through just weeks before and had washed out the last part of the road to get to the parking area, so we would possibly have to walk the portion to get to the place we needed to go. We had replied, *"No problem!"* because we were just in excited anticipation to see what God would do! And then, as we drove up this mountain in my big Yukon on just one lane so narrow you prayed you would not come upon another vehicle, we saw the red tape that barred us from getting up the last part of this massive incline. The road was so narrow it took massive teamwork just to maneuver and park the truck so that we could cautiously make our way back after our time on Prayer Mountain. Enthusiastically, we got our journals, Bibles, bottled water and my professional camera, and began the walk straight UP the mountain.

That climb was much harder for me on my body than for Kate, but I was trying not to show it at first. However, the incline was so difficult that I said to her, *"I need to focus on taking 20 steps with intention, then resting to breathe—so I can repeat."* She replied, *"Do you want to go all the way up? We don't have to do that, if you don't feel up to it."* Even though it was one of the hottest days on the calendar pushing 95 degrees and it would be hard work, I replied, *"No, I will make it. We have to go!"* I had made the decision to go the distance, even if I had to go with a burst of energy and then rest a while to start again. It took a while to get to the top, but we knew we would have plenty of time to rest because our plan was to stay a few hours. We were going to quietly sit, pray, journal and see how God would speak to us. We had come prepared!

What we hadn't come prepared for however were the conditions that were approaching the mountain. We were there only a few minutes and I said to Kate, *"Do you hear that?"* She listened and said back, *"Yep, that's thunder."* I knew that would have no impact on Kate—she had told me just the night before her parents always worried about her sitting on her front porch as a child wanting to be in the midst of the storm—lightning, thunder and all. She had told me how much she loved watching storms. On the other hand, I had progressed to the point where I could be out in them, but I still was not the type to want to be out in nature during them (much less on top of the highest mountain around)! So, we pushed the thought of the storm away because we were expecting God to tell us something on the mountain. We had come all this way and endured that climb, so we were determined that what needed to be shown to us would for surely come while we were on the top!

How wrong we thought we were! As the moments progressed, we could hear thunder getting closer and closer. I was looking straight up at the beautiful blue sky enveloped by white clouds thinking about my friend Thelma Wells and how I needed to reach out to her because her heart for others was so much in alignment with mine. Through these times with Kate, I knew we were all to connect for God's work. As I was still looking up with my head resting on the back of the Adirondack chair, I heard Kate say, *"The storm is getting closer."* I saw it too and, not more than even a few moments later, we knew we needed to walk down the mountain and get to cover. Together, we laughed while a little disappointed because we had only been on the top of the mountain for just a few minutes! We had nowhere near the time we had thought we would have to bask in God's message to us, thinking that in the quiet time on this mountain we would be the only ones there. When we had arrived there, just one person was leaving. And guess what? Her car was there at the top! We wondered whether she went around the red tape to take her car to the top because we had huffed and puffed our way up with sweat beading all over our bodies.

God revealed his message, just when we _weren't_ expecting it.

Kate and I packed our things and proceeded to make our way down the mountain. We began to talk and somehow the conversation weaved into the realization that my logo has a shield with a flame emblem that had originated back in 2008 and that her logo was the sword with a heart. I said to her, *"Wow, I just realized you are the sword and I am the shield. We need to study that more intentionally in the Bible when we get back."*

On this walk down the mountain I said to her, *"Wow, the path up the mountain wasn't so far after all."* She replied, *"It's always easier and shorter on the return."* It was in these moments that God was showing us so much more than we had realized. Kate said something about how we often want a God-experience, but we don't want to do the work for it. We started analyzing how she had been able to be up farther than me on the mountain because we had different paces.

This was an analogy of how our personal relationship with God takes work. And, because it is so intimate, we shouldn't compare ourselves to how others seem to be on their journey with God, because it is a unique process for each of us. She said, *"That is why we must go the distance! We thought God would show up on the mountain, but he has showed up in the journey!"* When she said, *"go the distance"* I had an epiphany right then and there. I said, *"Kate, this is why God woke me up from a dream and delivered the word ENDURANCE and the message GO THE DISTANCE."*

We processed all that God was revealing to us. That is when God spoke into my heart with an understanding I had never realized in all my 46 years of living. My voice dripped with such revelation when I said to her, *"Kate, here we have our stories of endurance to share. But, now I see God patiently endures to see in us what we don't see, so that we become what He has called us to be—that is the greatest story of ENDURANCE ever!"*

I continued to pour my heart to her and speak it to God as a thank you. God could have given up any one time out of all those times. When the Israelites were brought out of slavery and as soon as Moses went to the mountain, they turned their back on God after all He had done for them! God still forgave them, time and time again. Even after all those unbelievably disillusioning moments, when Solomon was given the gift of wisdom and then later began to worship other idols and when God saw the incredible sin in Sodom and Gomorrah, He still gave His Only Son to us! God has so much love, so much hope, so much belief and holds so much promise in us that He ENDURES forever! He GOES THE DISTANCE even when we have turned our back on Him! He GOES THE DISTANCE walking by our side holding to the journey that we must take to find Him!

We got to the truck and proceeded down the mountain! During that entire time, the storm never rolled in on top of us! This day of revelation was a process. We endured in seeking Him and He showed us that He is waiting for us to go the distance through the process while He will endure with us by our side FOREVER!

Psalm 136

¹Give thanks to the LORD, for he is good. *His love endures forever.*

²Give thanks to the God of gods. *His love endures forever.*

³Give thanks to the Lord of lords: *His love endures forever.*

⁴To Him Who alone does great wonders, *His love endures forever,*

⁵Who by His understanding made the heavens, *His love endures forever,*

⁶Who spread out the earth upon the waters, *His love endures forever,*

⁷Who made the great lights—*His love endures forever,*

⁸the sun to govern the day, *His love endures forever*

⁹the moon and stars to govern the night; *His love endures forever.*

STRATEGIES FOR BUILDING YOUR ENDURANCE

1. Think back to a time where you were battling a difficult situation. With a new perspective, how did God *"show up"* in your life to help you endure?

_____

_____

_____

_____

2. Do a search for the word *"Endurance"* in your Bible. What scriptures are you finding that could be your own personal sword to battle when it is needed? Write them down here.

_____

_____

_____

_____

3. On a scale of 1-10 (10 being the absolute best), how do you rate your personal commitment with growing your intimacy with God? Why?

_____

_____

_____

_____

4. What needs to happen to improve your relationship with Him?

_____

_____

_____

_____

5. What could be the ONE THING that you could do every day going forward to build your relationship with Jesus while strengthening your endurance muscle?

_____

_____

_____

_____

ABOUT TRICIA ANDREASSEN

Tricia Andreassen has a mission—a *"life calling"* she describes like this:

"My mission is to bring teaching and strategies to breakthrough challenges struggles, and obstacles that show up daily in our business and personal lives. Each person has a purpose and calling. I want to help as many people as possible discover what God has placed in their heart to do."

As a young entrepreneur, Tricia bought her first real estate investment property at age 19. Early on, she began to see principles and strategies that could be applied to help companies of all types build their brand, message and organization.

Andreassen started her Marketing, Advertising and Web Development company in grass roots fashion from the bonus room of her house with her toddler son literally on her hip and grew it into one of the most internationally recognizable companies within the target market it services. After almost 15 years as CEO, she sold her company to pursue her passion by expanding her personal coaching practice in business advancement into the fields of spiritual development and personal growth.

As her mission progresses, Tricia's growing life story continues to be told with a central message of persistence, resilience and faith woven into insightful strategies that heals the soul and transform results. Her passion is to creatively deliver, inspire, motivate and strategize lasting change through writing, speaking, teaching, the arts (including songwriting) in intimate gatherings such as workshops and retreats that focus on unlocking inner warrior strength.

For more than 25 years, Tricia has helped thousands of people with their lives and businesses. One of her companies, Creative Life Publishing and Learning Institute, was founded with the mission to help writers become authors and to bring teaching and training programs centered on faith, leadership, youth, parenting, business building, marketing and spiritual growth. Her business book Interfusion Marketing hit #1 in less than 5 hours and remained on the best-seller list for 59 weeks.

John Maxwell, the world's #1 ranked leadership expert, has certified team member Andreassen as both Speaker and Coach to teach leadership, personal growth and youth development programs. Her credentials also include an Executive Coach ACTP certification through the International Coaching Federation that positions Tricia to bring uniquely creative strategies to organizations, schools, ministry groups and leaders from all walks of life.

Contact Tricia:

- Website: www.MsUnstoppable.com
- LinkedIn: www.LinkedIn.com/in/TriciaAndreassen
- Facebook: www.Facebook.com/UnstoppableWarrior
- YouTube: www.UnstoppableWarriorWithin.net
- Twitter: www.Twitter.com/TriciaSings
- Instagram: www.Instagram.com/MsUnstoppableWarrior
- Radio Show: www.UnlockYourInnerWarrior.com

IT IS INTERESTING, LORD
By Tricia Andreassen

IT IS INTERESTING, LORD

It is interesting, Lord, how
*I think I don't know what to write about **ENDURANCE***
and then you speak into my heart.
*You show me that You have helped me **endure** so much.*
*Now, I am to praise You for what You have just used to **carry me***
***through endurance** to reach Your promise.*
So, I will share my heart with intimate vulnerability,
so that it may bless the heart of another.
I pray this, in Jesus' name, Amen.

God has been speaking to my heart about the transformational things that have been stirring under the surface in my life for many years that I will most likely share in a full book called *Miracle House*.

For now, I begin with fall of 2014. At that time, my friend Kristan posted on Facebook that she was raising money for Teen Challenge in Arizona to give back to at risk youth. Her son was there struggling with health issues after a serious accident in which his life was miraculously spared. It had been a long journey of surgeries. As if that wasn't enough, his brother passed away as well. God used all of this to bring him to a place where his life and health was restored at Teen Challenge.

Just a few months prior to this, I had recurring moments of pain that rose from deep down caused by things I had stuffed from my growing up years. You can only push things away or down for so long. I had even written a song about it in 2008 that had said:

'Rise up, stand strong
take a look around it all
you know what you gotta do

It's all inside of you

Push the pain of the past away
It's the start of a brand new day
Open your heart to what may come
It doesn't matter where you're from.

As I reflect over these last three years specifically, what I realize now is we must do more than endure layers of truth, feelings and pain that have built up for us to come through to the victory on the other side. Covering them up rather than dealing with them is not an effective use of endurance.

I had turned my back completely on God when I entered my college years, even though I had grown up in the church. Pieces I had put together in my mind led me to the conclusion that religion was hypocritical because those who claimed to be ministers and Christians were doing unthinkable things behind the scenes that no one wanted to talk about. It was an unspoken demand that stories of abuse of any kind (physical, emotional and sexual) were to be kept very quiet and never discussed. The more stories of shame I discovered (along with the abuse I experienced myself), the angrier with God I became and the more I mistrusted those who said they walked with the Lord.

I will admit endurance did serve me to a certain extent, but at the same time it bound me up in chains until I nearly suffocated. My soul wanted freedom so badly that it would ache for it!

In writing this story, I know that an experience of ENDURANCE is two-fold.

ONE, while I was unaware, God endured alongside me, holding me, waiting for me to call out to Him, and TWO, I was holding onto strength within me, trying not to quit, believing I could make it on my own. Over those years from as far back as I can actually remember I lived by the mantra, *"If it is to be, it's up to me."* I didn't realize that was only partly true because the filter I had put on this statement meant that God didn't really have anything to do with it.

Of course in my childhood going to places like youth camp would pour the Spirit of the Lord into me to show me that He was really there holding me and waiting for me, but then I would go back home and have to participate in the activities of the church where my mom pastored and I would become confused about how could God really be there when such sin was rampant. Being the youngest of three girls in my household, I knew when things weren't quite right but it was a unspoken law that certain things were to be kept quiet. However, when my immediate family got together, I (at as young as age 6) couldn't understand the anger, the fighting, the rebellion of one sister, and the quiet voice of the other sister who would not confront to keep the peace. It was that quiet sister (14 years older than I was) who would take every chance possible (when coming home for a visit) to pour love and light into me. But, I only saw pieces that were like broken pieces of glass that, if stepped on would become bloody and painful, taught me not to cause ripples of any kind.

I became the much needed entertainer—I was the Hopegiver, the Joychild who kept my dad calm as much as possible to avoid his angry outbursts. I had also taken on the responsibility of being the *"good daughter"* who held their hand, played the piano, put on skits, offered to play games and whatever else I could do to bring joy to the underlying shame, anger or uncertainty that those family holiday experiences (like Christmas) would bring. As I was growing up, more little things were unveiled to me that I didn't want to know. I can't remember the first time I was sexually abused. All I know is that, in the spring of 2015 while making love to my husband, I had an emotional breakdown where my husband held me while I was curled up like a ball on the floor (rocking back and forth sobbing uncontrollably from something hidden that had become so deeply rooted.

In 2014, I was forced to *"face the giants"* as co-author Kate Bancroft would say. When my parents made a decision to move back permanently from Florida just a few minutes down the road from our home, I began to ask questions that had been in the back of mind for years which resurfaced only to be buried again like a shameful game of *"hide-n-seek."* Yet, knowing that I would now be the leading responsible caregiver for my parents, feelings rose up within me that I became determined to find answers to.

This is truly why I say that *endurance* has been two-fold. I now know that God was seeing me through this time of unlocking memories from deep within me to interfuse strength into my own spirit to restore me to the beautiful creation He planned for me to be. In that summer of 2014, I approached my one sister (who has had many lifelong emotional problems) to ask her about being abused by my Dad. She proceeded to tell me things that I know where purposely hurtful to break any trust connection between my other sister and me.

I remember that day I asked her some questions. I was on my phone with my earbuds while walking into the grocery store. Things she told me were so upsetting that I walked around the store in a daze only to leave and not purchase a single thing. I drove home with such a feeling of pain that I felt destroyed. She had a history through the years of telling me the most hurtful things to abuse and scar me greatly—mentally, emotionally and spiritually. While growing up, I tried multiple times to be that supportive sister I thought I was to be. But, we rarely talked because I knew her abuse *could not only be* due to her mental issues, substance abuse and other things. Yet, I had questions about our childhood that needed to be answered.

You see, I was searching to find understanding. I had believed for my whole life that there must be a way that I could somehow break free. If I could find a way to make money and be in control of my decisions, I could get out of the environment that was so often unbearably terrible. Sure, I knew God was there, but, in my mind, it wasn't like He was watching over me. I thought, *"How could He be watching over me and taking care of me when such cruel things had been around me most of my life?"* Only now in my maturity, do I know that *He created in me a level of endurance that He would use to keep me moving forward!*

I say this because I distinctly remember in second grade going to Michigan to visit my sister who I thought was working at a mental home to help others (the one who I referred to from the phone conversation in the grocery store). I believe now that was perhaps just a story of some kind and I sincerely still don't know all the details because *"the voice"* became quiet. What I did find out is that she attempted suicide and ended up being in that hospital. My parents needed to see her and I was the only child at home (I am the youngest, 10 years younger than my middle sister and 14 years younger than my oldest sister). I remember taking my Holly Hobby suitcase on board the plane and my 3 small Holly Hobby dolls which were securely safety-belted in zipper pocket in front of me so they could view our trip. These dolls, my teddy bear Egger (given to me by my older sister who was like Wonder Woman to me) and my other stuffed animals were like my friends because at times I was extremely lonely being the youngest child. I don't remember much of the trip, but I remember staying in a home where (even at seven years old with limited understanding) I noticed that the folks living there were mentally *"different."* My sister was only 17 at the time and still to this day I do not know how she ended up in Michigan so far away from our family in Virginia and West Virginia. Many times I have asked my Mom things only to be told, *"I don't remember."*

Through those younger years, I only saw those pieces of broken glass. Those on *"the outside looking in"* saw this church-going dedicated family that sang, preached and ministered while something was always stirring underneath. At this moment while writing, *I know God put inside me a determination to want to live, to make my own way and to go the distance! I know that is how I endured through it all!*

When my middle sister was about 18 years old, I remember her knocking on the door of our 23 foot trailer in the middle of the night. She entered with a young gentleman who she said was her husband. They had eloped and he was studying in college to be a chemist. Clean cut and from a large family, he seemed to bring security to my sister. Perhaps that was why my parents let me stay with her the summer between my fourth and fifth grade year. My mom went for 6 weeks to Washington DC to learn computer programming for her job at the telephone company and I went to Tennessee to stay with her.

Both of my sisters lived in that town. My older sister and I were very close, but my middle sister would mentally manipulate me by saying, *"If you go to see her, that means you don't love me."* I remember being on the phone at times over that summer crying on the phone to my parents. My mom asked me if I wanted her to come get me, but I was this little girl who was afraid because my sister had convinced me that *"if I left, it meant I didn't love her or care about her."* During those living conditions in Tennessee, my sister's husband did the best he could with her issues, but I didn't understand the drama. I remember him throwing furniture all around the house in a rage over something while in a fight with her. I remember my sister was a babysitter for a three month old baby and I was left to take care of the baby while my sister partied at a friend's house or stayed in bed all day. I grew up quickly learning to take care of a three month old and at the same time take care of myself. That was when I developed an incredible fear of thunderstorms. On one occasion, I was left alone and lighting struck the tree in the front yard and I became massively afraid. I hid under the furniture until they got home. I was a 9 year old little girl, learning to care for herself because she knew she could not rely on anyone else.

I guess it was in those times my older sister would call and ask me to come see her that finally my other sister said I could go for an overnight visit. I was so excited to see my big sister as I thought the sun and moon set with her. She was the one who I felt always gave me stability. That evening we had dinner with her husband who was always friendly and social. I had even been their flower girl at five years old in their wedding ceremony, wearing a yellow dress with little white sunflowers printed and holding little white daisies in my hand. Those who looked upon me saw the picture of innocence, yet they had no idea of the reality behind closed doors.

That night after dinner and hanging out in the living room, my brother-in-law went downstairs to play pool. I thought the pool table was super! My sister was in sales and had this incredible big house. All I knew was living in a trailer park. It was like a dream being there. I bounced downstairs to watch him play pool and the next thing I remember was him giving me a French kiss. I was so confused, scared, turned and ran back up the stairs. I don't remember if I stayed that night or if I had Karen take me home the next day, but I kept this quiet not telling a soul. She would ask me to come stay with her while I was at Regina's, but I always said no because I was scared. I was living in what felt like an emotional hell that summer.

Somehow, I *endured* and returned home to my parents. Perhaps, it was when I told my parents some about living with my sister that summer that gave my Dad the clue to be mindful that I had a voice to speak things more outwardly. Perhaps that is why I don't recall abuse from him in those years going forward except moments of the emotional kind where he would lose his temper behind the steering wheel driving at 80 miles an hour yelling and my mom trying to calm him down, while I was in the back seat terrified.

Somehow I *endured.* There were times that I don't know how, but I do know that my older sister was someone that *taught me how to endure* as over the years I learned about the level of abuse she went through from my father, other friends of my parents and her first husband. I later learned that she also tried to take her life at age 14 years old, right around the time I was born. She has told me many times that I was the best Christmas present she could have gotten because I was brought home on Christmas Day.

In some instances, memories for me are blurred on timelines on when I was fondled by my uncle. After several times, I began to find my voice. At about 8th grade, I told my mom and dad about it. I remember how my dad responded like it was not a big deal. I felt he didn't go *"to bat"* for me. Even when my uncle knocked on the door to ask my dad to pray for him and I was there in the house watching him walk in, being welcomed into our home, I felt so angry and betrayed. I thought to myself, *"What parent would be so accepting—knowing that their child was hurt in such a way?"* These feelings were so difficult to comprehend but, opening up to my sister after her divorce from her husband that molested me, I was able to feel like someone loved me and things were not my fault.

My sister Karen moved to Blacksburg Virginia after her divorce, went to VA Tech graduating with honors, and later got her Masters. I lived with her most of those few years while I was in high school which was a saving grace. I know that God yoked us together to lift one another up and endure through our past. Together we had hope, determination, faith and commitment to see things through. I am so grateful for her today. Even in times of struggle in our personal growth journey and our understanding of one another, we know that God brought us together in heaven before we were born. This is how I know with certainty that, not only my mindset and actions created endurance, but God never left my side whispering to me to never give up and to know that my life was made for a purpose.

Reflecting upon this sharing with you, I am also reminded of the endurance of my dad and the grace that God has given him. When I first got the word *Endurance* in my dream, I had *one* part of clarity, but a deeper revealing came in the days ahead. My dad had been shopping in the department store with my mom and ended up falling, resulting in broken ribs. He was admitted to the hospital and then was moved to a rehab/nursing home facility to recover.

The *SECOND* revelation came when I was walking into the facility. I stopped in the restroom to freshen up and to wash my hands before proceeding to my dad's room. I love how God even reveals himself in the most interesting ways because as I was washing my hands I felt the Holy Spirit speak to my heart saying, *"You know you were thinking about the word **Endurance as going the distance being physical**, but there is the component of the **spiritual ENDURANCE** that must be shown."* I know this was revealed to me specifically in reflection of the day before where my mom and I went to visit my dad.

I remember walking in to his room and he appeared so weak and even confused. I helped him get up and dressed while talking to him. While in the restroom with the nursing assistant, my mom looked at me with tears in her eyes and said, *"He doesn't look good."* I was considerably worried because he looked like his life was slipping away in just a matter of days. That is when I prayed, letting God lead me. After he was seated in the wheelchair, I sat across from him in a chair facing him knee to knee. Looking at him straight on I said, *"Ok Dad, I want to see how you are doing...make sure that you are here with me. Your body can be weak, but I want to know how your spirit is and if you are with me right now."* In the last 4-5 years, my dad has lost his ability to speak effectively so he said through his stutter, *"I...am."* I continued on. I said, *"Okay Dad because we know that your body needs to heal, but your mind and your spirit are so important in your body recovering."* With a little humor in my voice I said to him, *"It's hard being here, around old people with that old energy. But you are only old, if you choose to think you are. God has a lot more for you to do and accomplish."* At 84 years old he looked at me and said, *"I am. I...know..."*

Over those next few hours, I took him for a walk and we stopped along the way to minister to people. He had the Bible laid out in front of him from the day before and asked me to read it to him. We talked about God's love. He shared about his physical therapy exercising. I poured into him all the love and support I could to bring an energy that could raise him up. We were there the entire day visiting with dad. I went to Walmart and got him some of his favorite treats, drinks and a stuffed animal of a parent kangaroo holding to its baby. I saw these other little stuffed animals and loaded up my shopping cart with them because I could feel how that home had so many that were not visited often and had felt neglected.

When I gave those to my dad, I could see the spirit of hope rise up in him.

We stayed with him until dinner time. I pushed him in his wheelchair to the table and we sat and visited while he ate his meal. I know God spoke into my heart reminding me of a process my sweet friend Jodi had taken me through on forgiveness just a year before. I was able to bring this process to my dad after this long day together and the reveal that the Holy Spirit within us is a catalyst to keep moving forward. My mom said her goodbyes to dad and was going to stop off at the nursing station and restroom before I was to take her home. That left me and my dad sitting there in the dining area and I could see the tears in his eyes and the regret of his mistakes through the years. The Spirit of the Lord surrounded us in that moment when I was standing next to him, leaning down to say my goodbyes. I said in that moment, *"Dad, I would like to do something with you if it's okay."* He responded by quietly saying, *"Okay."*

I let God lead in that moment. *"Dad,"* I said. *"I want you to repeat after me. I forgive myself."* I will never forget the look on his face and in his eyes when he looked up at me. Even now typing this, I am amazing how God stepped in and allowed me to spiritually coach my dad in that moment with pure love. He said with his stutter, *"I...forgive myself."*

Looking at him I said, *"Dad I want you to say it again for me."* He looked at me more determined like he needed to overcome and said, *"I forgive myself."*

With the Spirit of the Lord working through both of us, I said in a whisper still with my left arm around him looking down, *"Say it one more time."* He looked at me and said, *"I...forgive...my..."* And then instead of finishing he looked up to heaven and said, *"God please forgive me..."* with a plea in his voice. At that moment I said, *"Dad, God wants you to know that He loves you. He forgave you a long time ago. He wants you to realize that He has forgiven you. Just like Moses delivering the Israelites out of slavery, they didn't realize that they were free. God had saved them and they were free, but they still acted as if they were bound in chains like they had been for 400 years. God has set you free. He has forgiven you and He wants you to see what He sees in you."*

It was the next morning visiting my Dad again that the meaning of *ENDURANCE* was solidified. That day as we were together, he said to me stuttering through his words, *"Determination...I won't quit. I... have...things to do for God still."* Observing God renewing his spirit and watching his personal endurance to go the distance was an inspiration. Over those coming days, he shared that he had exceeded his steps goal for walking in physical therapy. He was so proud! The physical therapist commented on how he gave his all every time he went. He continued to fix himself up, dress himself and prepare for the day even while disabled with 4 types of arthritis and with those broken ribs. He had made a decision to *go the distance!*

As I watched his progress, I told him about the book on *endurance* and that I was going to dedicate the book to him. I found out later from a nurse that he was so proud and said to her, *"My daughter is writing a book about me."* And, you know what? It is a book about him and so many others who make a choice to go the distance even when all the odds are stacked up against them. Even though my dad fought his own demons, he continually took it to God and sought help from specialists, therapists and more from my sixth grade year through my adulthood. He could have said, *"I am broken. I have done things I am not proud of... I can't change."* But instead he chose to fight. He chose to work and to improve. He chose to face the abuse that he had experienced as a child. He chose to *ENDURE.*

Even through other chapters in my life journey which I will save for another time, one thing I know is God can help you as He has helped me! Through it all, He has been there and has guided me to choose endurance. That is why just a piece of my story is being shared with you right now. What may be looked upon as an old piece of glass is actually the strongest element that can cut through anything and has the ability to hold heat to ignite a flame. It is in our broken pieces that He creates you beautifully. He has put warrior strength in you that you may not know or may think was lost along the way. I am here to be a walking testament and reminder that *you must endure*, because my friend *God is not done with YOU yet!*

PERSONAL REFLECTION

_____

_____

_____

_____

_____

_____

_____

_____

_____

_____

_____

_____

_____

_____

_____

_____

_____

_____

_____

MY GIFT OF DYSLEXIA
By Desiree Anderson

MY GIFT OF DYSLEXIA

Endurance? A bit puzzled, I slowly hung up the phone.

My new friend had told me she is preparing to publish a book of life experiences that exemplify unusual endurance. A book about *endurance*? Recalling inspirational stories of people enduring unbelievable hardships, I began to see why she is so excited! She is asking selected individuals to contribute their stories and is hoping that I would write *my story* for her! *My story?* What hardships have I endured in comparison to so many others? My hand lingered thoughtfully on the receiver. Should I? Could I? Would I?

As the irony of my friend's request swept over me, a vision of the little-girl-I-used-to-be flashed before me. She smiled at me and winked, as a quotation came to mind:

> *"There is a choice you have to make in everything you do. So keep in mind that in the end, the choice you make, makes you."*
> JOHN WOODEN*

"...the choice you make, makes you." But what did I know about endurance? I decided to start with the basics--look it up! Miriam-Webster provided alternate meanings for specific aspects of the concept of endurance. It seemed a good place to start:

1: *permanence, duration*—the endurance of the universe;

Psalm 136:9 KJV, *"The moon and stars to rule by night: for His mercy endureth forever."*

2a: *ability to withstand hardship or adversity;*

John 16:33 KJV, *"These things I have spoken unto you that in me, ye might have peace. In the world, ye shall have tribulation, but be of good cheer, I have overcome the world."*

2b: *ability to sustain a prolonged stressful effort or activity*—as a marathon runner's endurance

Galatians 6:9 KJV, *"Let us not be weary in well doing, for in due season, we shall reap, if we faint not."*

3: *act or an instance of enduring suffering*—endurance of many hardships

Hebrews 12:2 KJV, *"Looking unto Jesus, the author and finisher of our faith, Who for the joy that was set before Him, endured the cross, despising the shame, is set down at the right hand of the throne of God."*

As I read these definitions, the meaning expanded into the exciting concept that every aspect of endurance is rooted deep in the character of The Creator, and is therefore foundational to every part of our lives!

ENDURANCE—the word crept into my mind, settled down, quietly but firmly waiting to be addressed. Other words slipped in, gathering around it—strong, brave words like choices, challenges, goals, determination, acceptance, commitment, effort, striving, sacrifice, self-denial. These words were followed by painful, hurting words like disappointments, embarrassment, failure, loss and pain. Then came dark, heavy words like limitations, fatigue, difficulties, trade-offs, troubles, temptations. *"Butterfly"* words drifted among them bearing beauty, strength, light, faith, trust, hope, encouragement, faithfulness, confidence, humility, courage. Picturing the word *endurance* surrounded by familiar words that had long been my close companions, I felt I was beginning to recognize a very faithful old friend!

What an exciting challenge! I thought about how, while there are some challenges we choose to accept for reasons that are important to us, we will also face many difficulties and trials that are not of our choosing. In either case, *"there is a choice we have to make"* in how we will respond to whatever challenges we may encounter.

"...the choice you make, makes you." The little girl appeared again, this time giving me a big, bright smile and a thumbs-up! The choice was made. We could, we should, we would! With God's help, I would write my story. I thought it ironic that I would be asked to write a story for a book, because for most of my school years, I didn't think I was big enough—or smart enough—to ever do anything important.

I was 5'0" 95 pounds. My grandfather nicknamed me *"Rinky-Dink."* I was plenty smart in most ways; but in some, I was clearly different from the other kids—like when I couldn't make my spoon or crayon work right unless I moved it to my left hand!

When my mother would say, *"Aim high"*, *"Keep on keeping on"*, *"Anything worth having is worth working hard to achieve,"* I would just smile and say, *"Yes, ma'am."* I was too embarrassed to tell her that I did work hard, I did keep on keeping on, but I just didn't seem to have the capability!

In my early grades at the Christian school, everyone worked at his own speed, so the difference wasn't as evident. Sure, the others were a few *paces* farther along, but I thought that was normal. It was hard for me to read, spelling was really hard, but I thought it was just as hard for everybody. Not until I moved to a public school in fifth grade did I find out just how different I was from the other kids my age! I most certainly didn't measure up to the teachers' expectations!

In sixth grade, the teachers decided who would move into middle school on the college-prep *"Advanced Diploma"* track and who would be placed on the *"Standard Diploma"* track. I, of course, was assigned to the lower track for those who were not expecting to go to college. That was until my mother learned of their decision. I remember my teacher being called to the office for a phone call and motioning me into the hallway when she got back. She said my mother had called and asked that I be considered to be put on the Advanced Diploma track. She wanted me to take the college-prep courses because she believed I would learn more by being motivated to keep up with the stronger students.

Aware that my mind worked differently than my peers', I wondered how I would be able to handle the more difficult courses. One thing was sure—I would have to work harder than ever before! I remembered a picture of my granddaddy holding up both his arms that were badly scarred from being severely burned in a house fire. He was wearing a broad grin—and a red T-shirt that said, *"Tough times don't last, tough people do!"* Standing in that hallway, I knew I wanted to be one of those *"tough"* people who would outlast even the toughest times!

Digging Deep

I loved sports. I played several and I was always the smallest player on the team. What I lacked in size, I was determined to make up with heart—and my faithful friends—extra practice and more hard work! To compete with my teammates, I needed to do a thousand more volleyball serves, shoot a thousand more baskets, run a thousand more sprints and swing at a thousand more softballs—all in an effort to be a valuable member for my team!

At this time in my life, I allowed myself to be defined by numbers. Every sport I played, every test I took and every pound I gained or lost was assigned the number that supposedly represented success. I prayed to God that I would somehow measure up to who I thought I was supposed to be. In spite of all my prayers and effort, I still fell just shy of the supposedly acceptable number. I couldn't understand what was holding me back! I was trying so hard! I studied long hours, making sure I understood the lessons. But somehow, no matter what I did, my test grades never reflected my grasp of the material.

That was until one evening when something happened that began to change everything! I was studying *Macbeth* for an exam when, seemingly on a whim, my mother offered to help me study by listening as I read the story aloud. I read aloud for a while, and then we discussed the plot of all the kings. As I read further, my mother correlated the story to that of Job in the Bible, how he resolved to keep trusting The Lord during very difficult times that were happening for no apparent reason.

We discussed the importance of allowing ourselves to be defined, not only by who we are in Christ, but by choosing to die to self-destructive desires and allow The Holy Spirit to live through us. (Who but my mother would use *Macbeth* to teach me how Christ calls us to allow Him to guide our choices.)

While taking the exam, after studying for it with my mother, I had a feeling of confidence that was different in me, greater than ever before. The next week, in Mrs. Arnold's fourth period English class, she was calling us up to her desk to give us back our tests. As I listened to my peers discuss the grade they made on the test, I was hoping nervously that I might finally have gotten a good grade. I had studied really hard—and differently—this time. This was the first time I was ever excited to get back a test! (I had set myself a goal of making the National Honor Society. For that, I needed an average of 85. However, as I lived in the 76-82 range, the honor society always seemed beyond my grasp.)

Finally, Ms. Arnold called me up to her desk. As I stood waiting for my paper, my eyes were drawn to a small black leather Bible that she kept on the top corner of her desk. Its torn corners and faded edges showed that it had been much used and well loved. I remembered her saying months before, *"A worn out Bible is the sign of a good man."* I don't remember if it had belonged to her dad or her granddad, but I remember being thankful for a teacher like her and proud of her unapologetic commitment to Christ.

At last, Mrs. Arnold put her glasses on the tip of her nose and tipped her head down just enough for us to be eye to eye. As she handed me my test, she smiled and said, *"Now this is the grade I expect for the duration of this semester."* What Mrs. Arnold did not know then—nor did I, until a few years later—was that I have dyslexia. I had just had my first glimpse into relearning how to learn!

Hardly daring to breathe, I went back to my desk and looked at my grade. Unbelievably, I had made an 87! A couple of my friends were not happy with their grade, and I overheard one of them whisper, *"Even Desiree made a good grade, so how could I not have made an A?"* As I listened to my friends that day, I realized that we were all fighting the same battle—measuring ourselves by numbers and standards set by the world.

Something happened in the classroom that day that was significant for many reasons. This time I did not measure my worth by the grade. I hardly noticed the 87. I suddenly felt closer to my friends than ever before and in a different way than I had felt with anyone. I realized that I loved people and that I cared about people who were hurting. I realized that I could choose not to allow the opinions of others to hurt me! Better yet, I could choose to show others how much Christ loves them; that He is painfully aware of our flaws and loves us unconditionally. That English exam, Mrs. Arnold's smile, and a happened-upon study technique marked a pivotal point in my life. I realized, for the first time, that I was capable of doing well in academics and I felt like a fishing net cast over me years earlier had been removed.

During the infamous study session with my mother, she also spoke of Moses being called by God to lead his people out of Egypt. Moses questioned his ability to speak to Pharaoh because he assumed it required an ability he didn't think he possessed. Moses asked God, *"Since I speak with faltering lips, why would Pharaoh listen to me?"* In Corinthians 1:26, Paul tells us that when Christ calls us, we need only make ourselves available to Him. He needs only that our hearts be willing to follow Him, no matter the cost.

Looking back, I think my mother must have taken the opportunity to work in that lesson. I cannot for the life of me find any correlation between Moses and *Macbeth*. I can only surmise that as a mother in tune with her child—and aware of my insecurities—she worked in the invaluable lesson of *enduring* difficult times, along with the importance of maintaining a healthy perspective when making choices that determine who we will become.

The most important lesson was making enduring commitments. I learned I should commit to small every day choices and to allow Christ to accompany me on my journeys, however long and treacherous they may be. I learned that he wants to be there with me. How fitting, in a world where we often feel like someone has failed us. We can count on his ever-present commitment to us with a love that embodies the definition of endurance.

Staying The Course

A couple years later, I was preparing to enroll in Mississippi State to continue my college education, and it was time to declare my major. I really wanted to apply to the nursing program, but was hesitant because I didn't know if I could handle the vast amount of reading that would be involved.

One day, my then mother-in-law, Maxine, and I were sitting on the floor of the hallway while the men worked on the water in the bathroom. I guess we were there for moral support because neither of us were contributing to the bathroom situation, except for stating that we were hungry and wanted dinner soon. Maxine had been a career nurse and was then a nursing instructor at the local community college. Of course, we got around to discussing my major.

"Desiree," she said, *"you know you are supposed to be a nurse, and so do I. When God calls you to do something, you'd better do it, because the alternative will never be pleasant. We all know you can do it. I think it is time for you to stop making excuses just because you are scared, and let's get this thing going."* (While Max is one of the most caring and loving women I have ever known, she does not mince words—we call her *"Sarge"* with good reason!)

I realized Maxine was right; my mind drifted back in time to a day just before I was to start my freshman year in college when an afternoon of shopping with a friend suddenly turned critical. While stopped at a red light, we were horrified to see an oncoming truck strike a boy in the intersection! My instincts outweighing my knowledge, I rushed over to where the injured child lay motionless. While we sat waiting for the emergency responders, I was consumed with a passion to help the boy—and with an overwhelming uncertainty of how to do so! My sense of helplessness became the root of my career decision. I would be a nurse.

I did struggle with the tremendous amount of reading in nursing school, but I had been prepared many years before—I knew what I had to do—work harder and longer than what was considered the norm. When others went home for the night, I stayed at Starbucks and studied for a couple more hours. While others slept, I got up at 0400 and prepared for the lesson we would study in class that day. I was used to working longer hours, but now that I was in nursing school, everything was different. I was actually learning how to care for hurting people. The reading seemed more like a privilege than a burden. Mostly, it was different because I was certain that it was The Lord's will for me to become a nurse and certain that He would help me deal with whatever I had to do.

Gut Check

In high school, there was a time where I started defining my achievements in terms of numbers that represented success. In nursing school, there were two more occasions where the Lord again used a number to get my attention. The first was when I was studying for a critical pathophysiology exam. I had begun to increase in confidence and had even taught some study groups because pathophysiology made sense to me. I taught the neurological section, and I knew it backwards and forwards. I failed the exam with a 62!

When I walked out of that room, after learning my score, I could not talk! I walked straight to my car, drove home and fell on my knees. All I could think about was: how I did not want to disappoint my then husband and his mother Maxine, the amount of scholarships we would have to pay back if I failed out of school and the fear of never becoming a nurse—never being trained to provide care to hurting people.

As I lay there on the carpet in our living room, my face covered with tears and sick to my stomach, I heard music! The TV was on and Jeremy Camp started singing *"I Will Walk by Faith."* The words permeated to the very core of my being: *"Well, I will walk by faith, even when I cannot see, because this broken road prepares Your will for me."* I made plans to go the next day to review the test with my instructor to see what had gone wrong and started preparing for the next exam.

Two weeks later, I was walking over to the testing center and praying for help on the exam. In my head, I thought, *"Lord, please help me make a good grade, so that I can have more confidence going into the final."* Before that thought even cleared from between my ears, I heard the Lord's voice: *"Is your trust in the number or is it in Me?"* I stopped short, almost got hit by a car and tried to gather my thoughts.

Wow! Ok. That came through loud and clear. I don't remember what I made on that exam. I don't even remember what my final grade was for the semester. But I do remember that fateful day when my unconscious became my conscience and I have never doubted The Lord again.

Then came the day, during the last two busy weeks of school, when in a classroom filled with chatter, I heard my name called and turned to see someone handing me an envelope. Surprised, I took it and opened it. The first words I saw were: *"Desiree: It is with great pleasure that I inform you of your induction into Sigma Theta Tau International Honor Society of Nursing."* Tears blurred the words and I had to excuse myself to run to the restroom to cry. I cried because I knew I did not earn that induction on my own. I was crying because I was thankful for the people who believed in me. I was thankful for the mother who took the time to let me read *Macbeth* to her and to teach me lessons I would not understand until years later. I was thankful for the teacher who was not ashamed of her faith and kept an old worn out Bible on her desk as an example to her students of staying the course even when life is difficult and for showing us that The Bible is our One True Guide. I was thankful for the mother-in-law who challenged me to see beyond my perception of myself and to go the distance—no matter how high the mountain. I was thankful for the group of friends who lived with me, enduring and encouraging my constant studying: Candace, Jessie, Christina, Tony, Angie, Matthew, Darilyn and many others. I owed a debt of gratitude to these individuals that I was sure I could never repay.

Fast forward 10 years. I am married to John, also a nurse. For the past ten years, he and I both worked at a trauma center in trauma ICU with some of the brightest, most caring individuals in the profession. Two years ago, I transitioned to the Emergency Department. It was there that I was faced with my most significant patient to date. Thirteen years in colleges, three degrees and ten years in the nursing profession had all been preparation for this one day *for this one patient*. It was my day off, but I was going to work to cover a two-hour gap for a friend so she could go to a ballgame to watch her daughter cheer. My Dad wasn't feeling well, so I asked if he wanted to come to work with me to be checked out. *"Yes,"* he said, already getting to his feet.

As we drove the few miles to the hospital, I knew it would be our last ride together. My Dad rolled down the window and let the wind blow on his face. I knew he was saying goodbye to this world. He was ready to go home to be with the Lord and his loved ones already over there.

As part of the staff, I could help care for my Dad that morning. His status changed quickly from bad to worse and soon we were at the crossroad. I asked him if he fully understood that instructing us not to put in a breathing tube meant that he would be in Heaven today with his mother, father, his brother and his grandson Devin. He smiled and nodded his head—yes! His last choice was a definition of who he was and how he lived. He chose peace and he chose quiet.

My Dad had plotted his own course. His journey was coming to an end. He had endured long enough.

Seasons of Life

As I pondered my Dad's life, I thought of how life is full of transitions.

I started asking myself these questions: Am I passionate about what I am doing in life? What do I have in place to help me develop personally and professionally? What are my daily habits? Are they beneficial in helping me reach my goals or are they distractions?

As I transition into my speaking and coaching career, I find myself being constantly reminded of God's call on my life and the choice to stay the course when challenges hit. As our sweet friend Julie stated, *"He did not call me to succeed, He called me to be obedient."*

Today, my passion is helping people remove the lid of their self-awareness and dispel their self-limiting beliefs. We are all capable of more than we realize, but we are limited by our belief in what we can see and ourselves.

I challenge you to walk as far as you can see, when you get to the end of your vision, you will see further.

Every day we must be intentional in our growth and how we cultivate our mind. James Allen, in his book *As A Man Thinketh* wrote:

"A man's mind may be likened to a garden, which may be intelligently cultivated or allowed to run wild: but whether cultivated or neglected, it must, and will, bring forth. If no useful seeds are put into it, then an abundance of useless weed seeds will fall therein, and will continue to produce their kind."

A good place to start each day is with Proverbs 3: 5-6, *"Trust in The Lord with all your heart and lean not on your own understanding. In all thy ways, acknowledge Him and He shall direct thy path."*

> *Look at yourself in the mirror and commit*
> *today to make those cultivated choices.*
> *Tomorrow, choose again!*

*John Wooden was the coach at UCLA from 1948 to 1975, and in that time, UCLA won over 80% of all of their games. From 1971 to 1973, Woodmen's UCLA team went an amazing 89-1. Wooden coached some of the all-time great basketball stars including Karee Abdul-Jabbar and Bill Walton. His influence on these stars went well beyond the basketball court. In addition to his success in sports, Wooden is also known for his short inspirational messages that have often been quoted by coaches, writers, and motivational speakers.

STRATEGIES FOR BUILDING YOUR ENDURANCE

1. What can you learn from this experience? What can you do differently to move forward?

_____

_____

_____

_____

2. What are the biggest things you've learned in life to date?

_____

_____

_____

_____

3. What advice would you give to yourself 3 years ago?

_____

_____

_____

_____

4. What daily habits do you have in place to help you grow as a person to reach your full potential?

_____

_____

_____

_____

ABOUT DESIREE ANDERSON

Desiree Anderson loves The Lord with her whole heart. She is a dedicated wife to John and a mother to Alex, Ashton, Trinity, Tyler, Kennedy and Daniel.

Desiree obtained her Bachelors of Science in Nursing from The University of Mary Hardin Baylor in Belton Texas and is a Nationally Certified Critical Care Nurse. She has also held a Certification as a Sexual Assault Nurse Examiner {CA-SANE} for the Sexual Assault Prevention & Crisis Services Program for the State of Texas. She is currently transitioning from a career in Trauma and Emergency Nursing where she dedicated herself to caring for the physical, emotional, mental and spiritual needs of her patients to a career of serving others through coaching, speaking and mentorship. Her goal is to lead others to explore the extremities of their perception of themselves and to encourage personal growth as a continuing way of life. Her goal is to help organizational leaders understand and increase their leadership effectiveness and to create unique strategies for Ministry teams, School systems and Hospital Administrators. She is also a faculty member of Unstoppable Warriors for Christ, a team of individuals who have answered the call to ministry of God's word as well as driving the global mission of bringing people hope, life skills and resilience.

Desiree is a Certified John C. Maxwell Executive Coach, Leadership Trainer and Keynote speaker. Her goal in life is to leave a legacy for her children of making a difference, with people who make a difference, doing something that makes a difference at a time that makes a difference.

Contact Desiree:
- Website: www.CLPLI.com/Desiree_Anderson
- Email: Deskron613@gmail.com
- Email: DesireeAnderson@IDLife.com
- Phone: 706-577-3958

A NEW DEFINITION
By Kate Bancroft

A NEW DEFINITION

The headache shut me down. I was taken by surprise by this one. It has been absent for many years and I rather enjoyed that. Why now? As I laid in bed, in the dark, eyes closed just trying to get past the pain, feeling sorry for myself, I was reminded that this was once normal for me. This monster sinus headache had returned, threatening to split my head wide open.

I had successfully come through a very difficult pregnancy with a healthy baby girl. Life was improving. Everything was falling into place. I was healthy and back to work. Or so I thought. One morning I realized that part of my left arm felt numb and no amount of rubbing was reviving it. I ignored it for a few days, but the spot seemed to be growing and soon it was my entire forearm. I could still use it, but it didn't seem to have the strength that my other arm did. I was scared. I was sure I was dying. I asked my husband if he would still love me if I was disabled.

My first trip to the doctor was a failure. They pushed my symptoms off onto my recent delivery and said that I must have pinched something during delivery. Right, I had a C-section! So we waited for improvements, but instead the numbness continued to spread. The left side of my face was going numb. It felt like my face was heavy. The right side would smile, but the left not so much.

Back to the doctor—this time I was scheduled for a wide range of tests. I remember during one of the tests, the technician kept saying, *"I don't know why you are having this test. It's obvious you have MS."* This is what I heard over and over the entire time I was there. I knew nothing about MS but knew from how he talked about it, it must be bad. Over the course of two years, I had approximately twelve tests done. Not one single test showed anything conclusive as to why my arm, face and now my leg was experiencing numbness.

So here I was, with two kids under the age of 5, with my entire left side compromised. Did I mention that I am left handed? I could still function but the strength was not there. My hand and leg would just give out without warning.

On this roller coaster ride of doctors and tests, the final straw was hearing a doctor give the diagnosis that it was all in my head. There was nothing wrong with me. I was just making it all up. He suggested a different kind of doctor for me. We walked away from seeking answers and decided we would figure out how to *"live with this"* ourselves.

Looking long term at my physical abilities, we built a house that, if the time came, I could manage on one floor. Stairs were not always kind to me. I accepted that this was just the way it would be. I wasn't the mom who ran and played with her kids. I was the mom who stood by and watched. I watched my husband and kids climb up Sleeping Bear Dunes without me. I watched on the sidelines for kickball and watched on the side of the street for bike riding. I remember my daughter wanting to learn how to do a cartwheel, something I was once very good at, so I showed her how, only my left arm didn't hold the landing. I crashed.

We knew nothing about why this was happening, so we didn't know how to stop it from progressing. If I pushed through, would I make it worse? Does pushing through make it better? The not knowing put us in a place of *"just trying to survive."* We became very good at adapting our life around my limitations. This is how we lived for years—in quiet resignation to surrender.

Writing this story through the lens of *endurance,* I truly felt like I failed. This was not the story I wanted to share. I would rather tell of how I never gave up and how I crossed the finish line covered in blood, sweat and tears. I would rather have been authentic in cheering you on, telling you to go for it, don't quit, and keep going. God had a different plan. Talking to my publisher the day I had the headache, she listened to pieces of this and said, *"You know this is the story you are meant to share."* To my amazement here it is. I began to question my *"why"* of surrendering to this giant I was living with. Why did I just sit down and take it? Why didn't I push harder? Yell at the doctor? I had people tell me *"It must be God's will"* or *"You have sinned and He is punishing you."* I knew I had done so many things wrong in my life, maybe deep down I did think I deserved it.

I definitely was living in a pit. In the book of Daniel, we read how he was thrown into a pit with lions and are amazed that he is unharmed. God was in the pit with him protecting him. Is it possible He is in the pit with me? In 2 Samuel 23:20, Benaiah chases a lion into a pit. Who does that? The rest of us would run the other way! I was expecting the lion to strut out, give a huge roar, shake his mane and be licking his lips but that's not what happened. Against all odds, Benaiah is the victor. God was in the pit!

In surrendering to this *"giant"* who was my companion in the pit, I thought it put me out of the running for *endurance.*

Endurance—you know, in it for the long haul, lifetime venture requiring time, work, determination, spiritual discipline and commitment.

The definition of *ENDURANCE* didn't seem to line up with how I handled my giant! Did my *"pit time"* somehow tarnish my testimony? In working through this project, I have discovered I had a wrong view of endurance. *God's view of endurance is Eternal* and *my view of endurance was Internal*—all focused on comparing my actions to others and judging them to be less than.

On an annual doctor visit, I was seen by a new doctor. She was quite interested in my condition and the tests that were done. She recommended, quite adamantly, seeing a neurologist. I told her I was over being laughed at and treated like I was crazy. Just going to stay in my pit with my pet giant! She took my hand and told me that she would walk this journey with me and would not stop until we had answers. This was the first time I felt validated in how my body was feeling from someone besides my husband. I talked it over with my husband unsure if I wanted to go through the roller coaster again. It was agreed that I would step back into the journey towards wholeness. I told God that I needed a sign from Him if this was the path He wanted us to pursue. Off to the Neurologist we went.

Sitting in the waiting room, I asked God for a sign. In the examination room, again I asked God for a sign. I was so torn. I peeked my head up out of the pit unsure if it was safe to do so. The giant was having a field day. All the horrible things that could be thought were going through my mind—I was dying, leaving my husband to raise our two children by himself, was going to be totally paralyzed with visions of being bedridden, all on automatic replay.

In the midst of my fear crazy cycle, in walks Dr. Fink. I had been asking for a sign, right?! The only way I can explain it is this way—when Dr. Fink walked into the room, the thought that *"he is one of God's people exploded in my mind."* Okay, I know there isn't a universal code of how to look if you are a believer in God. Peace seemed to have entered the room with him—the peace that passes all understanding. The voices of the giant were silent for the first time in years—no worry, no fear, just a knowing I was in the right place and God was right beside me.

The first test ordered was an MRI. I had had one several years before which showed nothing out of the ordinary. This new one however revealed something different. I had a quarter-sized cyst in the middle my brain. We finally had an answer! Crazy to think back at how happy we were having an answer that was in the middle of my brain!

Dr. Fink, in all his years of practice, had never seen a cyst cause the problems I was having. He asked me several times about headaches. People with this condition always have headaches. This is one reason why the Bible says we are to guard our minds—not to allow that which isn't truth to permeate our thoughts. Yes, I began to have headaches! Dr. Fink ordered several tests to gather information on the extent of the numbness then referred me to a neurosurgeon.

Our appointment with the neurosurgeon's team was amazing. Once again, I was listened to. His team explained what surgery would look like and what outcome I could expect. To hear that *the neurosurgeon had performed hundreds of these*" was reassuring. We talked about the MRI and I asked about the first one. It did show the cyst in the first one, but it was quite small. The surgery then would have been far more invasive and risky. Is this why I spent so many years in the pit?

We were told that the incision would go from my right ear to my left temple and I started to cry. I was more concerned that I would be bald then having my head cut open. Such peace covered us! Our moms were going crazy at the thought of all of this. My husband and I were so calm—it was like we were cocooned in calmness.

The surgeon called to ask if I wanted to go ahead with the surgery and to schedule the appointment. I had never really understood Jesus asking the man at the pool, who had been laying there for years, if he wants to be made well. He had to want it, right?! I always thought that it was a dumb question, *"Do you want to be made well?"* The answer should be, YES! Life has showed me that is not always the case.

Many people get comfortable in their situation and do not want to do the work to gain freedom from it. I fit into that group. I had resigned myself that my physical issues were just the burden I had to bear. I chose to walk away from the pursuit of answers and went into a pit. Now, I was being given a choice—Do I want to be made well? The decision was in my hands and only I could make it. I was being given the opportunity to be placed into the hands of one who had the expertise to fix my health problem, to restore the feeling to my left side, and to give me back the freedom to run with my kids. Just as Jesus asked the lame man *"Do you want to be well?,"* the doctor was asking me the same question—am I willing to take the risk to gain healing? Am I willing to climb out of the pit victorious over this giant?

Looking back at my *"why"* of choosing to live surrendered to this giant, I discovered FOUR TRUTHS about my *"pit"* experience:

First, *my time* in the pit was what was best for me. I had recently accepted Jesus as my Savior when this health issue arose. I was battling in my own strength and not even seeking His. I needed to learn how to lean on Him and to surrender every part of my life to His will. To study His word and develop a relationship with the One Who gave His life for me. God has always been more concerned with the condition of my heart. In our weakness, He is strong!

Second, *God's timing* is perfect. If we had continued to push, the surgery option would have been far more risky and untested. As Jesus communicated in the garden, God's will—His timing and way —is always better than ours!

Third, *your "pit"* time doesn't disqualify you from living a life of *endurance.* The lessons learned in the pit prepare you for the detours, washed out paths and closed roads ahead. In the pit, you are battle tested and gain confidence in God working in your life. Think for a moment how Daniel felt knowing God was with him in the pit with the lions and seeing the faces of the men watching as he emerged victorious. In the pit, our testimonies are forged. We are called to walk on this road of life to eternity and God never leaves us to navigate it alone. Paul says that we are to run the race set before us.

Fourth, *God is always at work* in our life. When it looks like nothing is happening, there is no breakthrough coming and all you hear is silence, God is there. Luke 1:37 becomes a message we desperately long to hear: *"For with God, nothing will be impossible."* Nothing is impossible with God. It is impossible for God to do nothing!

I took the step, reached up my arms and let God lift me out of the pit. The surgery went off without any hiccups and it was pronounced a success. Cyst was gone! The side effects from my surgery have all but disappeared. I still do not tolerate flickering lights well and monster sinus headaches show up very rarely. I have met several people who have had brain surgery; every story is unique. Each one had to face the question *"Do you want to be made well?"*. The answering of the question is the first step up out of the pit.

For some the question isn't *"Do you want to be well?"* I talk to women every day who wish they were this way or that way, but are unwilling to step into the process. I have been told that *"I am too far gone to make a new start"* or *"This is just the way my life is."* The question becomes *"Are you willing to be made well?"* If I had not been willing to be made well, my time in the pit (that was used for growth) would have turned into a prison from which I might never have been freed. Life lived through excuses of *"It's just too hard"* or *"I am just this way"* would have sabotaged all access to my hopeful future.

As I seek a closer, deeper relationship with Jesus, pieces of my heart are revealed, healed and restored. Am I willing to be made whole? To be transformed into His image? Of course, all who claim Jesus as their Lord should say YES. We quote 2 Corinthians 5:17, *"If anyone is in Christ, he is a new creation, the old has gone and behold the new has come."* The act of transformation is not a once and done.

Transformation does take a life time. There are THREE QUESTIONS that require our response:

#1 *Am I willing to die to myself?* To step away from my flesh and pick up His agenda. My habits, my thoughts, my wants…to lay it down at His feet and leave it there. This is an area of struggle for me—I *"lay my problem down"* and pick it back up again! Matthew 16:24-25: *"Then Jesus said to His disciples, 'If anyone desires to come after me, let him deny himself, and take up his cross and follow Me. For whoever desires to save his life will lose it, but whoever loses his life for My sake will find it.'"*

#2 *Am I willing to surrender everything?* Everything means, well everything?! To pick up your cross and follow Him. When one is crucified—they only face one direction, the Son. They have no other agenda, just the cross. They only have right now and make the most of every moment. What would it look like to live crucified?

Galatians 2:20, *"I have been crucified with Christ and it is no longer I who live, but Christ lives in me and the life which I now live in the flesh I live by faith in the Son of God Who loved me and gave Himself for me."*

Matthew 16: 26, *"For what profit is it to a man if he gains the whole world and loses his soul? Or what will a man give in exchange for his soul?"*

Matthew 6:23, *"For where your treasure is, there your heart will be also."*

#3 *Am I willing to do the work necessary?* From our first breath as a believer to standing in front of Jesus—this is *ENDURANCE*—to run the race set before you—your race, not another's race with all the crazy twists, pits and turns of life compared to you sitting down because you just cannot take another step right now. To allow Jesus to dig deep within you to reveal, uproot and plant; to leave your comfort zone behind to find yourself fully surrendered to His calling.

The journey of discovering *His message of endurance* through this portion of my life has led me to *a new definition of endurance:*

ENDURANCE is how you live between your first breath as a believer in Jesus and standing before the Father, surrendering your life for eternity, hearing the words *"Well done good and faithful servant!"*

STRATEGIES FOR BUILDING YOUR ENDURANCE

1. What changes would you make in your life if you knew it was possible? What has kept you from stepping into the process of change?

_____

_____

_____

_____

2. Is there an area of your life that you surrender to God but seem to pick it back up? Take an honest look at yourself and ask why you take it back. Read Galatians 2:20 and replace the "I"s with your name. Read it out loud! This is your statement! Now lay it back down at the Cross. The life you now live, you live by faith.

_____

_____

_____

_____

3. Read 2 Samuel 23:20, Daniel 6:16-17, Genesis 37:23-24 and Genesis 39: 20-21. How can you relate to these stories of being put into a pit? How did God show up in their lives? Can you see how God has shown up in the pit you experienced?

_____

_____

_____

_____

4. Read 2 Corinthians 5:17. Is there an area in your life that you are frustrated with the pace of the transformation process? Look back at where you started and read Psalm 23:6. How has God's Goodness and Mercy changed your life?

_____

_____

_____

_____

ABOUT KATE BANCROFT

 Kate Bancroft understands how to turn your weaknesses into strengths. Kate develops growth, brings hope and trains women who are fighting the giants of self-limiting beliefs and the food they use to mask the pain. She is committed to walking with these women on their journey to breakthrough. She celebrates that when a giant falls, the true treasure they are is revealed. Kate draws from her 30 plus years in ministry, customer service, business building and life experiences to impact and transform lives through her coaching, speaking and writing. Her retreats and workshops provide a space to discover the weapons needed to fight and win against the giants in your life.

Kate is certified through The John Maxwell Team as an Executive Leadership Coach, Personal Growth and Development Coach and Communications.

Kate is a recovering chocoholic and an eating disorder diva who lives down a little dirt road with the love of her life, her husband Brian.

Contact Kate:
- Website: www.SlayingGiantsWithKate.com
- LinkedIn: www.LinkedIn.com/in/Kate-Bancroft-967559104
- Facebook: www.Facebook.com/Kate.Bancroft.94
- Email: Kate@SlayingGiantsWithKate.com

MY LAZARUS EXPERIENCE

By Wendell Betts

MY LAZARUS EXPERIENCE

Jesus said, *"This sickness will not end in death. No, it is for God's Glory"* (John 11:4, NIV).

The purpose of sharing my story is to promote *HOPE*. I was born with Asthma and at the age of fourteen had double pneumonia. I never smoked. I have had a great life *"in spite of"* the disease. Hope coupled with a positive mind and focusing on what can be not what might be has kept me going. You can live the life you so desire but you alone must make the choice. No one can do this for you.

The date is December 4th, 2009: Our day, Our wedding day. We met four-and-a-half years before. This was the day we made our vows and I was feeling so blessed to have Sharon become my wife. When I watched her brother Mike walk her down the aisle, I had a very difficult time not to break down. She was so beautiful! I knew we were going to have a life filled with adventure! How I loved her—my angel! Life was right; life was good. We both knew *whose* we were and we were so ready for this day. Life was good!

One evening just thirteen-days later, as we were sitting in our own family room I could feel my lungs getting tighter and tighter. My lungs were shutting down and breathing was becoming very difficult. Between eight and nine o'clock that evening I had taken eight asthma treatments. Sharon looked at me and with much concern asked, *"Are you okay?"* I struggled out, *"No. I can't breathe."* She asked, *"Should I call 911?"* I say, *"Don't have time."* Struggling for enough oxygen to get the words out, I utter, *"Let's go."* It was as though the door to the tomb was closing shut.

Sharon was dialing 911 as she drove towards the hospital; we met the EMT's half-way. They worked on me for twenty minutes on the side of the street trying to stabilize me enough to get me to the emergency room. Sharon was calling her mother, *"Pray, please pray! Wendell can't breathe!"* She told me later how that, after only two weeks of our marriage, she thought she was going to be a widow. Her heart was breaking. I was not breathing. My heart was exploding in my chest. My head was aching, pounding from lack of oxygen.

As soon as we arrived at the emergency room, the doctors and nurses took over and started me on oxygen and an IV of prednisone. I got there in time once again. This was not the first time this happened, but Sharon's first experience with how rapidly things can deteriorate in the life of a COPD patient. My condition stabilized over the next couple of days and I was released over the next couple of weeks. Things were back to normal (normal for me anyway). You see I was diagnosed with severe COPD (chronic obstructive pulmonary disease) in 2001 and, at the age of forty-seven, was deemed permanently disabled by the USA government.

I went back to work, but for the first time in my life I understood how quickly life can change or end in a moment.

For the next year, I was repeatedly talking to God: *"What is my purpose? Why am I here?"* *"I want my life to be meaningful. If what I am doing is not in Your purpose for me, then I want to move on."* You see, I had a *"dream job."* I was selling motorcycles; getting to play with toys daily and getting paid for it. Who wouldn't want to do this? Who wouldn't want to be me? After a year of praying and asking, my answer came. I was laid off.

During March 2011, I went back to work managing a small used car dealership. I could feel my health deteriorating slowly over the months ahead and by June 2011, I had to stop working. I was put back on disability. I could feel my lungs getting worse and had a difficult time even walking now. December 28 was the beginning of six hospital stays in a two-month period; up to ten days at a time in the hospital; a few days home and then, not able to breathe; dialing 911, yet again. February 26, 2012 was the end of a ten day stay. My breathing capacity was at 23% and I was diagnosed with very severe COPD. It doesn't get any worse! We had our home equipped with a huge oxygen tank and an oxygen concentrator. I also had to have two small tanks at all times so that I could have oxygen hooked up to my nose 24/7.

Simple things in life became very difficult. Little things, like walking twelve feet to the bathroom, became hard. When you can't breathe, nothing else matters. This statement is so true. You don't even care if you eat. Sleep comes in broken intervals—one to two hours at a time.

At this point, I was on the strongest doses of medications available and taking ten to twelve asthma treatments a day, as well as oxygen. Life changed dramatically. The stress level on Sharon was traumatic. She never knew from day to day where I would be health wise. She didn't know if she would find me home passed out on the floor, possibly dead or taken away by ambulance, yet again.

On August 18th, 2012, hope returned. It was a hot humid rainy Saturday. Breathing was extremely difficult. Sharon has gone for groceries. I didn't have the strength today to go with her. Life totally sucked out of me. *"I am sitting in my chair. I can't breathe. My heart is pounding heavily in my chest. My brain is aching, crying for oxygen. I am truly having a bad day. I can't do this anymore. I don't want to* go on." I am talking with God. I said, *"Lord, if I did not believe in heaven, if I did not believe in hell, if I did not know Jesus was my Savior, then I would understand why a person would put a gun in their mouth and pull the trigger. Today, it hurts too much to live. Let me die. I want to go home."* At this point in time, the grave clothes were welcoming.

The Reveal

"Surrender yourself to the Lord, and wait patiently for Him." (Psalms 37:7, GWT)

I was sweating and could not breathe. In this moment through His love and mercy, God revealed Himself to me once again. But this time, it was in such an amazing way. I could hear the voice of God as He spoke so clearly, say, *"Wendell, I can do more with what is left of you than you can do with the best of you."* I had never felt Him so near to me as in that moment (before or since). I just threw my arms open wide and said, *"Okay God, this is Your deal. I am Yours. Do with me what You will."* Then He spoke one more time saying, *"Wendell, I am going to use your life to influence a multitude of people."* All I could do was weep. *"Thank you, Jesus."* I knew then that things were going to get better.

In John Maxwell's book *The 15 Laws of Growth*, he speaks of *"The Law of Timing."* And so, having recently become John Maxwell Team certified, it is now even clearer to me just how key this is. You see, God's perfect plan and time are not ours. I knew healing was coming but not when, nor did I know how. It was not immediate. No, instead my health continued to deteriorate and in October 2012, Sharon had to retire from her position at the hospital after thirty-four years to stay home and take care of me. I could no longer be alone. I needed help in everything that we take for granted, dressing, bathing—everything right down to the most mundane tasks. I could literally feel life draining from my body. That winter was very difficult. I was on so many medications that at times my body would literally shake uncontrollably just from the side effects.

I would get up in the night to go to the bathroom and cough or sneeze; Sharon would wake up to hearing a crash; finding me passed-out on the bathroom floor. I would hear her crying out, *"Jesus, Jesus, please! Jesus, no, no, no!"* On one of these occasions, our tenant heard her cries and came running. My life's strength and vitality was being drained from my body, my skin was now grey, my eyes had no color. My fingers and feet were always cold from lack of oxygen flow. This brought back memories of seeing my father two weeks before he passed and how I could see death as I looked in his eyes. When I looked in the mirror, I saw that look in me!

In March of 2013, I had to go for another PFT (Pulmonary Function Test). I had these tests every six months for years to keep a record of where my lungs were at. Sharon went with me. These tests had become very difficult because I was asked to push all the air out of my lungs, I would nearly pass out and literally have tears running down my face from the pain of this. Sharon was emotionally distraught as she watched me complete one of these tests. It was the hardest thing I ever had to do. Breathing had become extremely difficult. I called my pulmonary doctor and set up an appointment to get the results of the test. It was now early May 2013 and while sitting in Dr. Williston's office having conversation, I had to ask her, *"What is next? What can I expect? Where do I go from here?"* This was when she told me, *"Wendell, I can't tell you the time or when, but where your health is right now, the next time you get sick you will be intubated, put on a machine to breathe or you will die."* I responded back, *"Then I am going to die because I do not want to be put on a machine; that is not living; just let me go."* That is when the doctor said that I needed to go home and discuss with my wife and family how I wanted it to be, so they would know.

This was difficult. How do you tell the ones you love, especially your wife that you love so much and who loves you so much, what you were just told? Knowing full well the next time you get a cold, which always ended with me being hospitalized, would be your end?

The Fight Within, The Desire To Live And The Turn-Around

"For as a man thinks..., so is he." (Proverbs 23:7, NKJV)

It was in June 2013 when Sharon and I were visiting a church that a new-found friend had invited us to. Before service, another friend who was a nutritionist, came by. I had met him a few years earlier when I sold him a motorcycle. This was Neil Burchill. At the time, he had owned a local wellness and nutrition company. He said, *"I want to help you, Wendell."* My response was, *"I know you are very good at what you do, but I, we have no money for that in our budget."* He said, *"No, that is not what I mean. I need to help you. I want to help you."* He gave me his card and said, *"Call Jocelyn on Tuesday morning."* I did and we started working on healthier life choices. For a few months, we worked on a healthier eating program. I was losing weight but still on oxygen.

At the same service, Spencer Court, who had invited us to church with him, owned a local gym. He told Sharon and I we could use his gym and his equipment for free to do what I could *"if"* that would help us. At this point, I was not willing to quit. So, we would go to the gym three days a week. I would lug my oxygen tank in and crank it to five (the highest setting) and do three to five minutes on the tread mill and then sit on the bench in the lobby for forty minutes waiting as Sharon would go through her routine. Then I would go home and go to bed exhausted from the afternoon; rest the next day to go back every second day to do three to five minutes all over again. Thinking back, I wonder what people were thinking: *"This guy must be crazy. He looks like death walking."* I was fighting with every part of my being to *"be and get"* better. I could not quit.

During this same time when Sharon would mow the lawn, I would strap my oxygen tank on and get the whipper-snipper out and do the edging around our lawn. I would edge for three to five minutes, sit and rest in the mini-barn for five to ten, then do another three to five minutes work until I completed the job. This would take me most of the day for what should have taken twenty to thirty minutes. Even this was very difficult for me. And yet, it was as hard but even harder on Sharon as she watched me struggle for every breath. Death was not going to take me without a fight. Death had its hands full because I would not give up—not when God told me, He was going to use my life as an influence for others. I must admit though that there were trying times, when my thoughts would go to a place where I doubted that I had really heard from God.

Let The Miracle Begin

"Everything worthwhile is uphill." John Maxwell

August 26th, 2013 was the start of an unbelievable new life. Rob and Penny Laagland had stopped by like they had done a few times to say hello and to see how we were doing. This couple had been such a blessing, leaving envelopes with cash and always so thoughtful. This Monday night they returned and the blessing they left was far and above the greatest ever. They had no idea! They left us samples of coffee a friend of theirs was selling and asked us to try it for three days; they mentioned that if we wanted to know more to give them a call and left their business card. We really enjoyed the coffee, so three days later I called the number on the card. That night, the couple invited us to come to their home to talk some more. Looking back, this seems really crazy. Prior to this, I would shut down every mention of a MLM (multi-level marketing) business. I was a complete skeptic. I simply did not believe they were legitimate opportunities.

Sharon and I met at the couple's home with Rob and Penny who I had known for a few years. This time, I was not even phased by the fact it was a network marketing business. We were in a desperate place, both physically as well as financially. Our house was listed for sale and we needed money. There were times we had even talked about walking away from the home and letting it foreclose. That night, our friends showed us a video about coffee being the number two traded commodity in the world and oil being number one. Being a previous trucker and having owned eighteen trucks, I knew about oil. But, I was amazed at coffee being number two.

Looking back, I now see how crazy this must have appeared. If I can create a picture in your mind, picture me with my oxygen tank shooting life into my nostrils, I turn to Sharon and say, *"We can do this."* I continue, *"We can invite friends to come for coffee and ask them if they're interested in buying from us or if they're interested in making a few extra dollars."* We said, *"Yes."* Knowing we had no money, our friends Rob and Penny paid for our membership. Thus came the biggest blessing yet. It is always amazing how God works. I know at this point, you are saying *"So what, another MLM!"* You may even be thinking, *"Why am I even reading this?"* Please read on. The miracle is on the way.

Three weeks later on a Monday—yes, exactly twenty-one days after we started drinking our new coffee (which had an herb infused in it through the brewing process), Sharon was at work. I had to go down to the mini-barn to retrieve a screwdriver I needed to install an electrical outlet cover. This mini-barn was down eighteen steps and across the lower patio, down three more steps and then down a little slope. I had never been able to do this without my tank in either direction. However this day, September 15th to be exact, I went down and back, finished putting on the outlet cover and took the tools back down.

When I came back in the kitchen door, I leaned on the island and thought, *"My God, what just happened? I did this completely without oxygen!"* I could not wait for Sharon to get home to tell her! It felt so surreal! For days, we just stared at each other in amazement. This feeling went on for weeks. I have not used *'tanked'* O2 since that day! That day it was as though Jesus called out, *"Take off the grave clothes and let him go!"* (John 11:44, NIV)

Lazarus Realizes He Has Awakened

Thirty-eight days after, on October 2, I had to go for another PFT. This day, I will never forget! As the test progressed, Karen, the PFT Technician said, *"We will need to repeat this test. Something went wrong with this one."* I asked her what the problem was. She just shook her head saying that she had never seen this happen before. Karen was the senior tech and had been doing these since 1984. I asked her what was happening and she said the tests cannot be right because it showed an increase in my oxygen level and lung capacity. She could not give me the numbers as only my doctor could do that. However, I knew—a miracle was in the making!

I went to my doctor two weeks later and she told me my lungs had increased to 29% from 23% since the last test six-months prior. She was amazed at the results, but was not ready to accept how this miracle happened. Six months later, I went for another PFT and Karen was again amazed that my lung capacity was now up to 34%. Now, God had their attention. Six month later, another PFT, which had become routine for years now, showed that my capacity had now increased to 40%. This time the doctor wanted to know what I was doing differently since she could find no record anywhere that anyone had ever reversed COPD and come off oxygen without a lung transplant and decreasing my medications as well.

"…those that wait upon the Lord shall renew their strength." (Isaiah 40:31, NKJV)

In November 2014, I was contacted by Catherine Harrop, who is a well-known and respected reporter. Her CBC TV station was given my name by a mutually respected friend. Catherine had wanted to do a documentary on COPD and her friend told her about my story of how I had gotten control of COPD and was seeing this deadly disease reversed. She said, *"No one has ever done this."*

CBC met with us in our home and for three hours filmed our interview which was then edited to two-and-a-half minutes. This interview is available on YouTube, entitled, *"Wendell Betts, CBC News, December 2014."* My pulmonary doctor was also included in this documentary. She said that she believed the success was the result of the weight loss.

All through 2015 and into Spring 2016, my strength continued to slowly increase, even though my lung capacity leveled-out at 40%. In March 2016, I was approached by Organo, the coffee company, to try a new weight loss product they were bringing to market. I said, *"Yes."* I had become totally focused on becoming the healthiest version of me possible. Over the next ninety days from June to September, I lost an additional thirty-eight pounds and maintained this weight loss over the winter.

The following September I was asked to come and speak at an event in Tampa, Florida. My trip was paid-in-full by the company. On Labor Day weekend, I spoke to over eighteen thousand people at a conference held in the Tampa Bay Lightning Arena. This was a live simulcast to over fifty countries. That weekend, I was interviewed by three doctors who wanted to share my story with their patients. It was a great weekend. I now knew what God meant by *"a multitude of people."*

In October, I was connected to a friend with the New Brunswick Lung Association. Sharon and I met with Chief Executive Officer, Barb McKinnon. In November, I was invited to the New Brunswick Legislative Assembly and introduced by the Honorable Victor Boudreau, our present Minister of Health, as the *"COPD Warrior"*. This has now become my new nickname with the Lung Association—BREATHE. We felt honored to be invited as well to the Lung Association Christmas party. While there, I mentioned that my goal for 2017 was to *"walk the bridges."* I mentioned that I would like to do this as a fundraiser for *"Breathe."* On May 21, 2017 along with 40 plus friends, we achieved this amazing goal and raised over $5K.

My Story—A Modern Day Lazarus

According to recent statistics written in *Health Line* magazine, 80% of all COPD patients are long-term smokers, and yet, I never smoked. As a child, I grew up with asthma. More than once, I had suffered with pneumonia with several hospitalizations which left my lungs scarred.

In the eighties, my doctor strongly suggested I move to a warmer climate. And so in 1988, I took his advice and moved to South Florida where I lived seventeen-and-a-half years between Florida and Arizona. This USA move was, of course, before God placed Sharon in my life and things took the worst turn possible health-wise. The journey up to this point has not been easy, but I can say it has been worth it all just to see her smile and to know we are on this journey together! I am thankful just to be able to breathe in the crisp morning air and feel alive once again—Thank You, Father!

Once I could shed the oxygen tank and slowly increase my exercise routine, I began losing more weight. As of today, I have lost over 120 pounds and have gone from a 56 inch waist to my latest pair of silver jeans being size 38.

Father God is no respecter of persons. God will give us our miracle. However, we must also do our part and put some action with our belief to call it *"faith."* Otherwise, we may be right back to where we were before the miracle.

Now, having come so far, I have determined to get even stronger.

Through the past winter, I decided to step out and stretch myself as well as my faith. I walked two to five miles a day on a treadmill. This year, since January, I determined that I am coming off of as many prescribed medications as possible. Thus far, I am off three meds that I had relied on for many years. There truly is power in the *"spoken word."* Some say *"seeing is believing,"* but through eyes-of-faith, *"believing is seeing."*

The purpose of sharing my own modern day Lazarus story is to encourage *"your Hope"* to arise!

Are you or a loved-one suffering from a life-threatening disease? Has the medical community told you your ending will not be good? If this is your prognosis, then my story is *for you*! When you read my story as God's story, let HOPE enter in your heart! In so doing, your mind will then switch from negative thoughts to a positive thoughts which will open a brand new doorway for a great healing to take place in your mind, body and soul!

Lazarus came forth! It happened for Lazarus, it happened for me, it can happen for YOU!

Remember that when we come to the end of ourselves, it is then that God can begin! *Go the distance* with Him!

STRATEGIES FOR BUILDING YOUR ENDURANCE

1. Are you stuck in the negative mindset of what your Doctor told you?

_____

_____

_____

_____

2. Are you interested in becoming healthy? Body mind and soul.

_____

_____

_____

_____

3. Do you believe in the power of the spoken word?

_____

_____

_____

_____

4. Are you willing to do what it takes to be what God intended for you?

_____

_____

_____

_____

ABOUT WENDELL BETTS

 Wendell was raised on a farm with 9 siblings in a very rural area from New Brunswick Canada and as a boy had a dream of doing great things and seeing the world or as much as possible. Every time an airplane flew overhead he claimed it as his own and every time a big truck went by the house he would say it was one of his fleet of many rigs.

Wendell graduated from high school in 1971 in a class of 55 in which he was 52 on the list. He was told by many that he was very smart but did not apply his brains. Wendell started out 4 days after graduation in the cab of a truck and continued in that area of employment. By the time he was 46 he owned 18 big rigs and 22 trailers. He has travelled over 2 million miles in his life across North America and been in all forty eight lower states and seven provinces. Wendell hasbeen blessed in many ways.

In 2002 the American government deemed him permanently disabled and was diagnosed with severe COPD, Chronic Obstructive Pulmonary Disease, and his lungs at that time were at 42% breathing capacity. In 2012, Wendell was diagnosed very severe COPD and put on Oxygen 24/7. The average span of life after being put on o2 is 6 to 9 months. Wendell has chosen to be the COPD WARRIOR not for his benefit but so that others will somehow understand that with a positive mindset and faith in one's own self and a willingness to do whatever necessary we all have the ability to change our outcome and become better.

Wendell is the Warrior for the cause of the less fortunate who the medical system has given up on and created a belief that there is no hope. As long as we can breathe at all there is HOPE. Wendell is also a certified John Maxwell member as well as an international speaker.

Contact Wendell:
- Website: www.CLPLI.com/Wendell_Betts
- Facebook: www.Facebook.com/Wendell.Betts.9
- Email: wdsebetts@gmail.com

I AM ERIN'S MOM
By Jeanette Brewer

I AM ERIN'S MOM

"As (Jesus) passed by, He saw a man blind from birth. And His disciples asked Him, saying, 'Rabbi, who sinned, this man, or his parents, that he should be born blind?' Jesus answered, 'It was neither that this man sinned, nor his parents: but it was in order that the works of God might be displayed in him.'"
John 9:1-3 NASB

There are some events that you know will change your life, and there are events where things will never be the same again. Marriage is like that and so is having a child. For me both of these occurred in the same year.

I was married on October 1st and by the 15th, I was pregnant. My husband was finishing college and I worked in downtown Philadelphia. I was going to have a baby. I was naive and scared. I felt trapped in a situation that I could not escape. I bartered with God to allow me to have puppies instead. I wasn't ready to be a parent yet.

My pregnancy adventure began with a visit to the Obstetrician to confirm the obvious. Within a few weeks, we got to hear the baby's heartbeat. My nervous giggles made my belly shake so much that we could no longer hear the heartbeat. By December, we were forced to change doctors because the first practice no longer took our insurance. By January, I had transferred to another practice. There were tests run and I was anemic. I was given prenatal vitamins with iron and the morning sickness got worse. The baby was growing at a good pace. I was gaining the right amount of weight. Bagels and strawberry milkshakes for breakfast. Grilled cheese with tomato for lunch. I craved broccoli with cheese at weird times of day and night.

As a mother, the feeling of having a living and breathing being growing within you is both amazing and frightening. However, this event in April or May while working at my desk had significance to me later. This particular day, my baby decided it was a good day to turn and lay sideways. I was extremely uncomfortable. I had heartburn. I really wanted this child to finish the turning. So I began to encourage the child to do so by pushing a little on this side then that side. At one point the baby's foot stretched out between my rib cage and my skin. I could see the outline of the foot. So I began to tickle the foot with my finger. After a few moments of tickling, the foot retracted and the turn was eventually completed. I sighed with relief.

On June 5th, my husband graduated as a Physician Assistant and we decided to move to Ohio before the baby was born. His family lived there and would be a good support for our growing family. We received permission from the OB practice that it was safe for me to travel. The baby was not due until the 26. Everyone knows the first baby is always late.

We moved in with my husband's parents. I went to visit my new OB. He reviewed my medical records and we arranged where the child would be born. I visited the hospital and the new birthing wing.

As I sat in church on Father's Day (June 17) the contractions began. They persisted throughout the day but were not very strong. I was able to sleep through the night. However as soon as I woke up, I was immediately aware of contractions. They continued the whole day. My husband decided that it would be a good day to trim the hedges around his parents' property. At sunset, he was exhausted. But so was I. The contractions were five minutes apart and getting stronger. These were not going to go away. So we went to the hospital to see how things were progressing. They sent us back home.

I couldn't sleep. The contractions continued. We went back to the hospital at daybreak. They wanted to send me back home. I really wanted to stay until the child was born. They consented.

In the afternoon and although I was in labor, I had not progressed very far so they began giving me Pitocin to help the contractions. This mama was getting tired. I have now been without food and sleep for 32 hours and having active contractions. My husband was now asleep in the corner of the room. By 5 PM, as my husband was peeking under the sheet, my water broke with a splash. Then things began moving quickly. My breathing patterns through the contractions were old and boring by now. I wanted to push. *"Oh no, not yet,"* said the nurse.

They rushed to put the stirrups in the bed and they got them backwards. *"Do you have the left one?"* *"No, don't you?"* *"No."* *"Wait..."* The nurses were running around my bed like a three Stooges movie. Yuk, Yuk, Yuk. They put my legs in the stirrups, and told me not to push.

They were able to get the doctor in the room. He checked and said I was ready. He gave me permission to push through the next contraction. The baby's head was crowning. I closed my eyes and pushed. The head was facing my rear and had to be maneuvered differently for the shoulders. After the shoulders, the baby slipped right into the doctor's hands.

"We have a neuro tube defect here!" the doctor commanded to the team. A hush fell over the room. I was confused because I had not seen the large bubble on my child's back. The neonatologist was called to give care to the infant. The Apgar scores were taken. The placenta was delivered. The stiches were sewn. There was much activity in the room but all was done in silence or near silence.

I asked, *"Is it a boy or girl?"* *"I don't know."* I thought to myself—what do you mean, you don't know? They had to peel away the blankets to find the genitals. Yes, no one had looked. No one had charted that information. *"You have a little girl."* *"Hi Erin!"* I yelled across the room breaking the silence. I turned to my husband who looked pale and frightened. *"That is the name we selected, right?"*

My husband had seen the large sac on her back. His first picture of our child was of her deformed back. Meanwhile his parents, brother and sister-in-law were in the waiting room. What would he tell them?

They rolled our well-swaddled child over in an isolette. I saw her briefly, a beautiful face smacking her lips like she was hungry. But I was not allowed to feed her or hold her. I beheld her face for only a few minutes before the protocol determined what was done next.

God and I had been wrestling for the last nine months. I had already come to understand that God had chosen me to be Erin's mom. I knew that God had given me this child for a purpose. He would work out the details. It seemed surreal. What is a neuro tube defect? What does that mean? No one said. Everyone pointed to her trip to Children's Hospital and they would be able to answer our questions.

My husband filled out the paperwork and followed the ambulance to Children's Hospital. He would not return that night. The in-laws would not come to visit me. I was left in the private room at the end of the hall to rest and sleep. I did neither.

Sometime in the middle of the night, I walked down the hall to the nursery to look at all the babies. The nurse asked which one was mine. I stated that my child was at Children's Hospital. But I stood there in awe of the beautiful children that filled the room. Although I am crying as I write this, I did not cry at the time. The

Holy Spirit gave me a peace that I cannot explain. I went back to the room at the end of the hall. I wrote my baby a note. I was very glad she was now born.

The morning arrived I had been given my discharge papers. My husband was there to pick me up and told me that our daughter was in surgery. *"If we hurry, we can get there by the time the surgeon is finished."*

As we sat in the surgical waiting room with my in-laws, the surgeon came out to tell us the outcome of the surgery. *"She will walk. She will run. She will be able to bear children."*

He showed us a chart of the newborn's spine. He pointed out that her spine had not developed normally. She had myelomeningocele, one of the most severe forms of Spina Bifida. At birth, she had a sac on her back about three inches in diameter. The sac was filled with spinal fluid, spinal nerves and tissue. The sac had a dime size hole in it at birth, but had not leaked very much. Her chances of infection were low but they would be watching for signs of meningitis. The surgeon had dropped the nerves into the spine, made repairs and closed the sac.

"She will have a horizontal scar at her bikini line. She will have some paralysis in her feet, lower legs, and bowel and bladder functions." (But wait a minute. I felt her kicks. She stretched out her leg. I tickled her foot. How is that possible with paralysis?) He continued on with his well-planned explanation.

"Her head circumference will be measured daily for signs of hydrocephalus. If her head grows from increased spinal fluid, she will need another surgery to put in a shunt that will drain the fluid from her brain and into her abdomen. (He paused.) When she is ready, she will be moved to a room on the fourth floor and you can see and hold her later this afternoon.

Do you have any questions?"

That seemed like a silly question. *"Yes, how will this work out? How will I know what to do for her? How will we pay for this? Just for starters. How does this occur? Did I do anything wrong to cause this?"* I asked.

"Spina Bifida is a genetic defect that occurs around the 11th day of gestation. The spine is the first thing that forms and her genetic code caused the spine not to form correctly. Many with Irish ancestry have this genetic codes but it can occur in any family and any race," replied the neurosurgeon.

He then asked my husband, who had been in the Navy, if he had been exposed to Agent Orange. He answered no. The surgeon asked if anyone else in our families had spina bifida. There was no one that we knew. He reassured me that I was not at fault.

The social worker came and we signed more papers to receive financial assistance and make sure that our child received the care she needed. I wanted to try to breastfeed. A lactation nurse arrived and arranged for a pump to be delivered to the hospital. The nurses would use my milk before giving formula when I was away from the hospital. I would be able to nurse when Erin was back in her room. She gave me a card so that I could call if I had questions or had difficulty getting Erin to feed.

This was not what I signed up for. Every parent says this at some point in the years of parenthood. If you haven't yet, you will. The picture of what parenthood looks like is too glorified by Hollywood. However, my name is not Mrs. Cleaver or Jill Taylor.

First of all, I wanted to love my daughter and treat her like a child. I would take the challenges as they came. The social worker thought that I *"was not understanding the severity of the birth defect."* I told her that I did not know much about spina bifida but I was going to learn. I just needed to know what I needed to know for today. I needed to feed her, change her, bathe her and love her first. The other stuff would come as needed. She backed off and understood where I was coming from.

Erin was in the hospital 10 days. She did not need to have the second operation at that time, but another girl born the same week did. During the first few days, my husband went to the hospital library trying to learn everything he could about spina bifida and what it was. He had a stack of articles four inches high. I learned to breastfeed my daughter.

In conversations with my mother's family, we discovered that my mother's oldest sister had spina bifida and died in 1934. My grandparents never knew what it was and she never had corrective surgery.

We saw the staff at Children's Hospital every month for the first year. There was a parent support group to share resources and information. We went to conferences. We learned to catheterize our infant at two months. We learned to give enemas. We exercised her feet and legs. We played peek-a-boo and patty cake.

She did learn to walk with the help of orthotics (braces) to support her ankles. She played soccer. She took ballet and gymnastics. She got a pressure sore from riding a Big Wheel. Once, while standing at a window, I saw Erin stand on her tippy toes. Something I never thought she would be able to do. I cried.

As parents, we advocated for her needs in daycare and school. We carried extra clothes in our cars and extra catheters in our cars, our purse and wallet. We taught her how to catheterize herself. We trusted school professionals to help in kindergarten and first grade. We did a lot of laundry. The need for emergency medical paperwork for visits to grandma's house was covered. We dealt with prejudice: the private Christian school that did not want a handicapped child in their school. We talked them into taking her as a student and then regretted it. I learned not to be shocked that people were ignorant. I became an educator to all who would listen.

We lectured medical students on parenting a child with disabilities. We watched for bullying. We asked Erin to compete with the others in her class according to her abilities. We did not expect the world to change because of her challenges, but we did praise her ability to do all that she could do. If she couldn't do something and we could modify it, we did so she could be included. We tried not to punish her for things out of her control.

She loved to swim. She loved to write stories. She loved to play the flute. She broke her leg ice skating. She made lifelong friends. Many of the same things you wish for your kids or try to protect them from.

Erin had five surgeries by the time she was twelve. She grew into a lovely young woman. Her challenges continue as an adult with disabilities. In her first semester of college, she was nearly four hours away. She had a medical emergency and I could not have access to her medical information because of HIPAA. There is nothing worse that feeling powerless like that.

My days as a full-time parent flew by. My hope waxed and waned during those days. It wasn't always easy, but God was there from Day One. God only gives good gifts. I learned to be patient. I learned that there are things out of my control and that there are things that cannot be fixed. *I learned that there is beauty in brokenness.*

Today Erin is married with a child of her own. Childbirth was not easy for her. But having her own child fulfilled the final declaration of prophecy spoken by her neurosurgeon. She still struggles with her challenges and limitations. But she has a determination that does not quit. I do not know how her story will continue but I am excited to see her story unfold before my eyes. I am blessed to be Erin's Mom.

"Love puts up with anything and everything that comes along; it trusts, hopes and endures no matter what."
1 Corinthians 13:7 MSG

NOTE: all children with disabilities are unique and each story is different. There are many children with spina bifida who have very different outcomes. *God bless each of you as you live out your own story with God's help!*

In 1991, Bruce Carroll had a song on Christian radio called *"Sometimes Miracles Hide."* In the song, the lyrics say:

> *Sometimes miracles hide and God will wrap some blessings in disguise*

> *And you may have to wait this lifetime to see the reasons with your eyes'*

> *Cause sometimes miracles hide...*

"Now unto Him that is able to keep you from falling, and to present you faultless before the presence of His glory with exceeding joy, to the only wise God our savior, be glory and majesty, dominion and power, both now and ever. Amen."
Jude 24-25 KJV

Be a blessing and be blessed!

STRATEGIES FOR BUILDING YOUR ENDURANCE

1. Has there ever been a time in your life, when God's plan did not make sense to you? How did you handle that situation? How did that experience strengthen or weaken your faith?

_____

_____

_____

_____

2. There are times when we need to blame someone for events that take place. What is your reaction to the John 9 scripture that states that sin was not to blame for the man's blindness, but so *"the works of God might be displayed in him"*? Is that still true for today?

_____

_____

_____

_____

3. Has there been a time that someone spoke words over you that you wish had never been spoken? When my obstetrics doctor declared, *"We have a neuro tube defect."* He was calling together the experts we needed to care for Erin. He was shocked too. He truly meant no harm to my spirit by declaring my child's defect. The medical team was busy caring for her health instead of looking at her gender. But I will always hear that voice declaring her entrance into this world as such. The planned *"It's a boy"* or *"It's a girl"* was taken from me. How do you handle it when words are declared over you that are untrue or may cause you distress?

_____

_____

_____

_____

4. People handle events in different ways. My husband wanted to gather as much information as he could get his hands on. I wanted to study my baby and learn what worked best for her. We both benefited by our differences. How do you handle the curveballs in your life? Do you take them one day at a time or do you run to the experts to give you advice or tell you how it will be?

_____

_____

_____

_____

5. Some years later I also went to the library to get Information on how to better care for Erin. I also learned that many mothers of special needs kids suffer from depression which comes from prolonged grief. I thought I was crazy. What was I grieving? I was grieving the dreams I had for my child. I grieved the loss of income and savings spent on repeated medical expenses. I grieved in silence because to me it sounded like whining and self-pity. Some are grieving the life that they won't have because of extended care of a child that may not become independent as an adult. My grief seemed petty compared to theirs. I learned it was okay to grieve any of your losses. Who can you call that will allow you to speak without judgment? To whom can you be that friend that listens?

_____

_____

_____

_____

6. Does your church or organization have a way for parents' of special needs children to worship or get out for a while? What have you done for them lately? Have you called to check on them to see how they are? A sincere *"what can I do for you today"* goes a long way.

_____

_____

_____

_____

_____

ABOUT JEANETTE BREWER

Jeanette Brewer is the mother of two adult children and two grandchildren. She holds a degree in social work from Eastern University. In 2016, Jeanette became a John Maxwell certified speaker/ trainer and coach. She says her greatest adventure so far was home educating her two kids through middle school and high school. When God calls you to do a task He gives you what you need to complete it; however, at the time when stepping out in faith, you may not be aware that it was the best decision. But walking by faith is always a good decision.Jeanette's website is under construction and is not available at the printing of this story.

Contact Jeanette:
- Website: www.CLPLI.com/Jeanette_Brewer
- Facebook: www.Facebook.com/Broken2BeautyCoaching
- LinkedIn: www.Linkedin.com/in/JeanetteBrewer
- Email: Brewerj22@gmail.com

GIFTS OF GROWTH
By Jacquie Fazekas

GIFTS OF GROWTH

Most people do not seek out pain. As human beings we are content with pleasure. Life is good when we are laughing, smiling and enjoying life. So many things in life give us pleasure, whether compliments, success, sex, alcohol, drugs, decadent food or comfort foods. Have you stopped to think if these things help us grow? Or just make us feel content?

What in your life has really propelled you to grow?

If you work out, do you push yourself through the extra pain or do you quit before the legs become painful? If you endure and push through the pain, you become stronger.

If you struggle with self-confidence, avoiding facing your fears just keeps you paralyzed in self-doubt. However, when you step out and face your fears and learn from failures and pain, you grow in self-confidence.

The biggest and smallest moments of pain and suffering in my life have propelled me to grow much more than any pleasurable experiences ever did. It is only through deep reflection that I understand and appreciate the significance of my painful experiences and what gifts of growth they were. I grew each time when I endured through the pain.

Life Lesson - Keep The Faith

My struggles started early in my life. I was born with asthma and was often hospitalized. Consequently, I was not as active as the other kids and battled being overweight as a child. I was a curious child and was constantly discontented and restless in school. Fitting in with my peers was a struggle. It was painful many days. I would cry to my mother and ask why I did not fit in. She would simply say that my time would come, but it would be a while. My self-esteem suffered from the beginning of my early years. I tried to compensate for it by overachieving on everything I did. I was a model child and got the best grades. I would do all sorts of things that would make me stand out.

After getting sick in 7th grade, I lost a lot of weight and eventually started to model. I entered a beauty pageant in 8th grade and won! These achievements were only bandages to cover the pain and suffering I felt daily. None of these things shifted my self-esteem. It was not until 8th grade, I started praying to God for guidance on what He wanted from me, constantly asking Him why I did not fit in. I went through life judging myself and judging others.

Throughout my high school and college years, I succeeded academically, volunteered, started a debate club and work while in college. I projected that I was going to be successful to others, but did not feel that genuinely about myself. For years, I endured the pain of feeling different. At the heart of the pain was that I did not really love myself. I would spend many nights praying to God to help me understand myself and what purpose He had for me. I kept the faith in Him asking that He would guide me toward my purpose.

Life Lesson – You Cannot Love Another Before You Love Yourself

My life journey continued in typical standard progress. After college I got married. I was starting my career and was enjoying a lot of quick success. The success numbed my self-sabotaging thoughts. I still did not love myself, but I had convinced myself that being successful would make me feel better. Unfortunately, it did not.

After 6 years of marriage and lots of fun, I was plateauing.

It was time to have kids. I had told my husband I would not stay home with the kids. He decided to stay home with them as I continued to chase the work that was an addiction. I say it was an addiction because like a typical addict, I needed my fix of work and success in order to keep me from spiraling into depression. As I said earlier, I was simply avoiding myself.

Losing sight of balance in life, after having my 2 boys, I quickly found myself spiraling out of control. Work consumed me and there was little time for my spouse, my kids or myself. I made a job move with another company and relocated my entire family. In an effort to continue to chase success, my marriage ended and it was all my fault. Now, lonely and with two young kids in a new city with no support, I was faced with learning how to be a single mother and keep my career. Learning how to juggle and multi-task would be my new challenges. It was one of the most painful parts of my life.

I did not love myself, blamed myself for the failed marriage and struggled not knowing how to be a mother. I defined my worth through my career, but that was all on stall. Raising young babies by myself without family support or friends around was not easy, especially juggling an intense career that required travel. I quickly told myself I would endure on through the pain. I would prove it to myself and others that I could be a successful mother. This is the first time I committed to serving others and not myself.

The struggles were many! God gifted me with people to come into my life for a moment, for a few years or for a lifetime to help me endure the struggles of raising my boys alone. I remember saying to myself, *"God gives you what you can handle."* So I persevered on. There were days I said, *"What is God thinking? I need a break!"* Despite the pain and struggle, I continued to trust in God every step, in order to endure and grow as a mother and a career woman. I learned to seek out God's support, guidance and love, when I could not do it on my own.

Often, as addicts, we need to hit rock bottom to do our part in the rebuilding of ourselves into the person that God intended us to be. It is at the lowest points and most painful parts in our lives that we find the only one to turn to is God. It is during that stage He asks us to forgive ourselves and learn to love ourselves. Enduring the painful reality and learning to forgive yourself is when the growth comes and transformation happens. Love is an inside job first!

Life Lesson - Let Go Of Your Ego And Trust In God

As a mother and career woman, releasing control to God was tough! Despite my struggles to learn to be a good mother and continue to have a good career, I did not give the credit for the rebuilding of myself to God. My ego grew as others praised my success. I lost focus on His support and love along the way and never really faced my true self. Still not truly learning the lessons of self-love and releasing ego, it took the *endurance* of more pain and suffering for me to awaken to the fact that God is in control and I was not.

There were many significant struggles that I endured and that propelled me to growth. One of those struggles was when I did not get the promotion I thought I deserved. I was doing well in my career. I thought I was ready to handle the new position. It was another excuse for me to not love myself, so I continued to struggle with my self-worth for a long time after. My ego was bruised. What was wrong with me? I endured the pain of poor self-esteem and kept asking God what I was to become. After, additional career stumbles, I eventually learned that it was my ego making me feel negative, holding me back from self-love and that my career and position did not define me as a person.

After all these years, I finally learned that I had allowed my ego to control me. Societal comparisons, others opinions, and judgment of self and others kept fueling the ego. I needed to learn to find myself, have trust in God guiding me, stop judging myself and others and relinquish ego.

Now, every morning, it has become a daily practice to remind myself that I must relinquish my ego and trust in God every day. Over the years, since this lesson was learned, I can truly say that every time I let my ego overshadow my actions, I stumble. Daily, I am reminded in my stumbles that I must trust.

Life Lesson -Your Health Matters: Mind, Body and Soul

It was in 2009 that I was shaken beyond belief in my faith. I had a seizure and cardiac arrest at age 41. I was stressed out in my life, although everything seemed to be going right. I had just moved to a new job, relocated to a new city with my two young boys. I was promoted to Vice President of Merchandising, a position I had been seeking for years. I had been self-medicating to numb the stress for years. My self-sabotaging, self-medicating behaviors were many—drinking 12 cups of coffee a day, working into the night before bedtime, drinking at night to relax, not sleeping well long and no exercise.

I was still juggling my boys schedule as well. Clearly, what I told myself to justify my behaviors was my ego talking. I had lost sight of my faith and once again had not really tackled the lesson of learning to love myself. I had significant self-sabotaging behaviors, but did not recognize them.

It was in my darkest moment that God came to shake me! He told me that I had not really learned the other lessons of faith, relinquishing ego and self-love. I had been simply pretending and

He knew it. It took God really slowing me down, for me to reflect on my past and really start my journey of knowing myself and loving myself. God wanted to remind me that He was in control and that my health mattered.

A person cannot achieve and fulfill their purpose without health of mind, body and soul. A person cannot love others without loving themselves first. From that moment, I found myself propelled into my life learning journey. I continue to endure the pain of reflecting on past history, the pain of looking at myself in the mirror and the pain of not being in control. Enduring and growing through pain is full of blessings of self-discovery, purpose and love.

Life Lesson - No pain, No gain

A few years after my seizure, I was doing well managing my health. I was still juggling a fulfilling career, but was entering into a turbulent time raising my middle school boys. My faith was strong and I often found myself praying for guidance on how to handle the typical growing pains of kids. All the power struggles that happen with kids as they assert their independence was taking a toll on me. My boys were growing up and trying to find their way with friends, relationships, drugs, alcohol and school studies. The pressure was enormous on us all.

It was at this time, that I fell into love with a man. It was a quick love affair that resulted in a quick marriage as well. The relationship was a struggle from the beginning, but I was determined to make it work. I was not going to have another failed marriage! Falling back into *"I'm in control mode,"* our struggles worsened. It was only when I found myself knee deep in verbal abuse that a switch went off in my head. God had allowed me to be in this situation to continue to teach me a lesson.

Early on, I endured the abuse, sacrificing myself in the process. My boys witnessed the suffering and struggle and could not do anything for me, but love me. The verbal abuse went on for about 24 months. Throughout that time, the boys experienced their own learnings from the relationship. As family and friends continuously asked why I was still with him, I would always reply, *"I do not know the lesson God has for me yet."* Staying strong in faith, I endured through the pain. It was on my mother's death bed in hospice that she revealed to my sister the lesson I was to learn and the purpose this man was put into my life. She said he was meant to come into my life to teach the boys respect. I was to learn *"self-respect."* She said he had done his job and he could go now.

Two months later after my mother's death, I was overtaken by a simple struggle with my husband. Like a bolt of lightning, I became aware of the learning. He was envious of me and my boys, so he would put me down to build himself up. All my life, I had been experiencing people like this around me and I would allow it. When I would love and respect myself, the abuse would end. Without the pain, we cannot really sustain the learning we are meant to experience. Enduring the pain for 24 months was worth it! The results that I feel from it are life changing! My faith is stronger. I love myself. Endure through the pain to grow yourself!

Life Lesson - Faith Over Fear

Life went on after my divorce. My boys were in high school and living life! They were slowly spending less time with me, choosing their friends to be with. As typical teenagers, they would push the limits and I would have to set boundaries. The nights were lonely and often stressful, as I lay awake wondering if they would be home on time or whether I would get a call in the middle of the night. Unfortunately, there were other parents that got the calls. I was spared. I struggled with worry and my selfishness, thanking God that it was not my child. But what if it was my child one day? That was my real struggle. Would my faith be strong enough to overcome the pain?

Having raised my boys since birth by myself, I always felt that I needed to be in control. As you know, God tried to break me of control, but it did not work when it came to my kids. My oldest boy graduated and went far away to college. Like any parent, a panic attack comes on and then worry and fear set in. It took me months to build my enduring faith in God. Only when my faith became stronger than my fear could I sleep at night. My faith was really shaken when my last son went to college. In a constant state of prayer, I found myself stressed and worried most days. Then one day, I was struck by the words *"Thy will be done."* The words would repeat in my head for hours, days and nights. Let Thy will be done! That was it! Faith will overcome fear every time when you truly let Thy will be done! God was in control all the time!

Life Lesson – Happiness Is An Inside Job

Once the boys were at college, enduring the loneliness and quiet of my own thoughts was tough. I had always been busy, stimulated and fulfilled through others. It was only during my early childhood that I can remember the silence and creativity of my thoughts. It was painful then and painful now. However, I knew that God had some more lessons to teach with the pain I was feeling. Days would go by and I would pray for insights into the lessons.

I felt I was being called to serve and do more for others than I had time for in the past. My priorities were shifting. I had not made myself a priority. Self-love was a struggle every day and happiness too. A false sense of happiness was once defined by my kids, my family, by my job.

It was in the quietness of my own thoughts that God was able to tell me that *happiness was an inside job. Happiness would be found in being present in life.* My new lesson was now being revealed. Endure the silence of your thoughts and there you will find happiness. I have learned to enjoy being by myself and my thoughts. It has helped me to better love myself. Once again, you cannot find happiness or love unless you find it within first.

My prayer for you: *ENDURE*

When you have no more energy, rest and let Him power through.

When you have no more smiles, let one more curve of your mouth point up.

When you have no more patience, breathe and accept His assurance.

When you have no more appetite, take one more bite knowing you must be nourished to serve.

When you have no more love, trust harder and love harder.

When there is so much pain and little pleasure, endure one more moment, for your relief will be swift.

When you have no more confidence in the world around, the next step you might take or the future of your purpose, rest assure you have the greatest support and master plan being written for you with your every breadth.

Just endure and trust in Him.

In this journey, I am discovering the power of serving others. Success is but an ego focus. Serving Him and being significant to another is doing something worthy for God. I have lived much of my life in pain, but now understand that as I endured and grew through my pain, I got stronger so I could serve better. It is by sharing my life lessons that I hope I serve you on your journey. Each of us have our life lessons to endure and grow from. They are *GIFTS OF GROWTH* for your journey ahead!

STRATEGIES FOR BUILDING YOUR ENDURANCE

1. What has been one of your biggest growth experiences in your life?

_____

_____

_____

_____

2. What were the life lessons you learned from it? Reflect.

_____

_____

_____

_____

3. What is a situation you keep experiencing? What lesson do you think God is trying to teach you?

_____

_____

_____

_____

4. Why do you think you are repeating the situation?

_____

_____

_____

_____

5. How do you propose getting through the situation to learn the lesson?

_____

_____

_____

_____

6. Make a list of all the repeat experiences you can remember and when you conquered each. What was the common thread?

_____

_____

_____

_____

ABOUT JACQUIE FAZEKAS

Jacquie Fazekas has a passion for helping others find their purpose and passion. Through her struggles, she has always had a positive and resilient attitude. Despite the failures, she grows and she lives her life passionately every day, encouraging others to live positively too. She understands the power of overcoming failure and fears. She knows by encouraging others to endure the pain and overcome failure and self-doubt, their lives will be positively impacted.

She was born in Canada and moved to Naples, Florida when she was 13 years old. Since then, she has lived in many cities throughout the USA and travelled globally. Everyone around the world struggles and each person has their unique lessons to learn. With her passion to serve others, she is seeking out other ways to serve more people in a greater capacity. Passionate about holistic health and wellness, she shares her illness experiences with others in hope of sparking more awareness about the importance of living a holistic healthy lifestyle. Today, she is an active Hospice volunteer and mentors many young professionals she has touched over the years. As a Certified John C. Maxwell International Coach, Speaker and Trainer, she seeks to continue to serve others in their growth journey, meeting them where they are today and encouraging them along their way.

Contact Jacquie:
- Website: www.NowRealCoaching.com
- Website: www.JohnMaxwellgroup.com/JacquieFazekas
- LinkedIn: www.LinkedIn.com/in/Jacquie-Fazekas-82824b41
- Facebook: www.Facebook.com/JacquieFazekas
- Email: Jrfazekas@gmail.com
- Phone: 479-366-2838

IT'S WHO I AM
By Alyssa Harrington

IT'S WHO I AM

Imagine a world that's black and white, like an old movie, but no musical ques to tell you how to feel. The music is replaced by faint whispers to alert you, while the rest of the world hears loud sounds. You didn't know it, but your hearing had been severely damaged from ear infections every other month for the first five years of your life. Think of the antibiotics pumped into your little body. Let's just say you'd be smaller and the vital chemicals needed to keep you emotionally stable for the rest of your life were stripped away.

Let's take it one step further, imagine your school life. You're a child of average intelligence with perfectionist and overachieving traits. You work hard, you're even a self-taught lip reader, but the teachers take a permanent marker and write across your forehead, *'stupid,'* *'never going to succeed'* and *'impaired.'* Obviously, I'm speaking figuratively for there's no way that would all fit on a child's forehead. Luckily, you only hear their words a small portion of the time.

When you're almost six, you're plopped onto the surgery table where the doctors use tubes to open your ear cannels allowing your hearing to improve. It's only then you hear birds and the rumble of a car engine for the first time. You shock your mother as you mimic the sounds, because she didn't know you couldn't hear them before. And now you want to know their names. Let's take a deep breath—together. Now that the foundation is built, I want to welcome you to the rest of my story.

Likely by now you've figured out that public school was not for me. We had a hate-love relationship—mostly hate from it, and love from me since learning was my cup of tea. I didn't understand the harm of my teacher's words, but I was blessed when in grade three there was a parent in my class (she was there for her special needs son). At the time, she was also my after-school babysitter.

She informed my mother of what was happening, and advised her if I stayed in public school her little girl would be broken because my teachers were detrimental to my learning. This was my normal. I didn't know it was wrong. All I knew was my mom was taking me out of a school that deemed me incapable; that had sent me out into a yellow tinged stairwell with another student instructed to read to me.

I clearly remember the day she took me from that school. I eagerly awaited her as my teacher handed out the geography tests, soon coming to me. I glanced at the clock wondering when mom would come and save me from the evil test. I was beginning to panic. *"I didn't study enough!"* My heart raced as I picked up my pencil. Then like a superhero my mom came swooping in, and whisked me away. She never said I wasn't coming back. She just took me. And I left willingly. Anyway, I had no one to say goodbye to. No more isolation, a fresh new start.

 I was excited to leave, because mom said I was going someplace better. She moved me to a Christian school, where the teachers warmly welcomed me. Instead of entering half way through grade three, my mother worried about my reading and math so she held me back and I entered half way through grade two. Little did I know the torment, bullying and isolation I had felt in public school would come rearing its ugly head after my shiny *"new kid"* label wore off.

By the time I was nine, I realized something was wrong with me—that I was broken. I thought God had made a mistake. I chased after affirmation but could only witness the world lodge another knife into my chest. I was attention seeking to a fault, but all I really wanted was to be seen. Yet, I placed myself in the line of fire for their harsh words which they claimed to be jokes—crybaby, tattletale, *"Can you hear me?"* stepping back, *"Can you hear me now?"* The rest of their words were mumbles, because God had, as I thought, stolen away most of my hearing. This was all His fault. I cried easily. He made me too emotional. I sought out my teachers to stop the bullying, but God allowed my bullies to be so deceptive that all the teachers, even the ones who cared for me as though I were their own child, were blinded.

Even when the bullies struck me down, I had become so consumed with needing to be seen I believed they would change but they were incapable of it. My desperation was so high that I would do things out of character. I spoke my first curse word, I gossiped, I was cruel on the odd occasion to other classmates, all because I was tired of being invisible. They had me desiring acceptance so much that I was willing to leave my morals behind. Yet, doing all this didn't bring me into their favorable sights. Instead, they launched their *"jokes"* like arrows *more* often. How could I have known that (as an elementary student being trained by the world to seek acceptance from those around me)? I carried that unfortunate lesson with me all the way to grade twelve. My classmates by this point had been so cruel to me for so long it became their habit. They didn't know it then, nor do they know it now, but they tortured me with isolation.

At the beginning of grade twelve, a new student entered our school. He was three years younger than me. But now that I look back, I know God sent him to be the friend I needed. At that time, though he didn't know it (yet I'm sure everyone else  did), I had the biggest crush on him. He, in my opinion, was very attractive, kind-hearted, shy, but his one downfall was his lack of height. But, he made up for it with a great set of wheels that he was always rolling on. Yes, he's in a wheelchair and has a great sense of humor about it too. His name is Josh, and over the years he went from being a crush to one of my dearest friends. He was also my *"prom"* date in grade twelve. There he rolled over my dress a few times, couldn't get his wheels over the floor lights and flipped, but I know without him I would have felt isolated more than ever. God gave me support right when I needed it. I just didn't realize I should have thanked God back then. God and I were still getting to know each other. To me, He sat in the sky watching as if I was a TV drama.

Let's jump back for a minute to before prom. One of my wonderful classmates decided it was his duty to inform me I should be thanking them for making me into the person I was. I was so stunned I actually whispered a confused thanks. What I should have said was *"Thank you for breaking me, making me feel less than human, isolating me so I could understand loneliness and know a darkness that made me want to quit life on many different occasions over the ten years I've been your classmate. Thank you for never building me up and, instead, standing behind one girl who orchestrated it all because you wanted to be liked just as much as I did. You just did it better. So, thank you for teaching me that life sucks, and sometimes people are cruel. Yes, you helped shape me, but in the most negative ways possible."*

What they will never know, unless they happen upon this book, is that they pushed me to the brink. They made death look like a sweet escape. On one occasion, I wrapped my fingers around a metal pointed nail file, thinking *"I wouldn't have to listen to them. I could just slip away."* I had to force myself to find a reason not to. One of the first reasons to live that came to mind were my youngest cousins—triplets. I had occasionally cared for them with my aunt and grandmother for about three years. I couldn't leave. It would hurt them. I threw down the nail file with tear filled eyes. *"I wasn't going to do it. I'm not strong enough."* The dramatics of it all gave me a sense of comfort thinking I had merely been searching for attention—again. I wouldn't have done it. Yet, I am not so sure now. That scares me.

There would be many more times over the coming years when those dark thoughts would come back with a vengeance. The times when I was driving alone I would see the concrete divider heading into town from my home, or a ditch, and think, *"It would be so easy. I just have to let go."* As quickly as those thoughts came I'd remind myself that it was my mother's car. If I didn't die, I would have to face her after wrecking her van. Those were the only thoughts that stopped me. I would love to say that it was knowing my loss would make my family sad, but that wasn't a natural thought. For all those years, I had thought I was living because I wasn't strong enough to end it. But I was wrong. I was strong enough to not give up. I couldn't quit on anything, including life!

My mother knew it was bad, but didn't know how bad. She had spent most of my elementary and middle school years watching me escape to my room after school to cry. I would never tell her what had happened. I kept it to myself. I probably thought, if I didn't talk about it, it wouldn't seem so bad.

I never thought to turn to God. Instead, I cried out asking why or I just cried. All I knew was He had made me so different, so broken, so unlovable, so needy. He had given me so many negative attributes. I never stood a chance at normalcy. I was only allowed to dream of the high school life I saw on TV. Never once did I think God hadn't done any of it. Never once did I think that Satan had slipped his cruel fingers into my life to drive a wedge between us, making me see Him as cruel, distant and unloving. I was so angry with God—I cried out to Him asking why, but He never breathed a word. So, as I felt He did to me, I turned my back on Him too. I put on my Christian mask and walked the way I knew would make my parents proud.

Sadly, I was raised in a Christian home. I know what you must think, *"How's that sad?"* Let me explain: It's sad because I was raised in the way to go, but I walked how I wanted to. I had become a Christian mostly out of fear and because I knew it was expected of me. I prayed the prayer and wiped my brow after my baptism thinking, *"There, I'm safe."* As the years passed, I felt angry, lonely, helpless and broken. Even after God granted me back most of my hearing with a miracle at the age of fourteen and surgery at eighteen, I was still angry. He was the One Who had let people label me, and let that label be my identity. And then with the miracle and successful surgery, He destroyed my label. He changed my world. I didn't want to change, but He made me.

I moved on to university, doing what I thought my parents expected. I pushed to make good grades, but they never compared to my brothers, Micheal and Matthew. I sought desperately for who I was, putting my effort into basketball, which I had played since grade seven, and had received Athlete of the Year in grade eleven. I made it to the Championship with my team in grade twelve receiving MVP (Most Valuable Player) award. I should have felt confident, especially playing for the University ranked first in their division at the time. But instead, I still felt I wasn't good enough. Once again, God tore off that identity, just like my hearing-impairment, and in my second year I didn't play.

The feeling of depression, low self-esteem and desperation gave God the opportunity He needed to move me again out of a *"public university"* into a University in Moncton, N.B. It was a blessing because, in my second year there (fourth year all together), I roomed with two wonderful girls. One played on the basketball team with me which is how we ended up rooming together. The other was a friend of hers, Meaghan, not the basketball player, who has especially become prominent in my life. We built a bond that no amount of time can change. She has been a blessing from God in my times of need, cheering for me, crying with me, feeling my joy and encouraging me continually to trust in God. I hope I have done the same for her.

I graduated with a Bachelor of English degree with a concentration in Creative Writing. To add the cherry on top, my Korean homestay sister took me to South Korea for our two-month summer vacation. I never thought I would fall in love with Korea like I did. That summer, God revealed to me my next step in life. I wanted more than anything to skip over my Education degree and stay, but mom told me I had to come back. She said I had been accepted at a University in Canada and therefore God obviously wanted me to get an Education degree first. So, I flew back to Canada with Junyoung.

I started the Bachelor of Education program full of hope. I was going to be the best teacher! I got my practicum placement and I watched my dream crumble. I made it through most of the year, but on the last leg of my practicum my dream was burned. The school and my practicum teacher informed the university that I was detrimental to the students' learning. It was rather ironic since it was the public school system that was detrimental to my learning. Now, I didn't know what I was supposed to do. The University asked what else I wanted to do. I foolishly told them I dreamed of being a writer and they, in turn, more foolishly responded, *"Why don't you focus on that and just go get published?"* I was shocked. They thought it was that easy—that I could just walk out the door and BAM! Instant publication!

After that, I let both dreams die. Why die alone, right? If it were not for a very special professor, Mr. Sexsmith, I would have quit altogether. But, he gently pushed me along with his kind words that were full of hope and I graduated. I received a Bachelor in Education without the teaching certification, but I replaced that with an Advanced Certification in Teaching English as a Second Language.

I had achieved so much, but had lost my ambition. I did exactly what the university had told me to do—if I became a teacher, I would take whatever job I could get. But now, I wasn't a teacher and I took any job I could find. I ended up working at GoodLife as a part-time Motivator, a fancy word for a secretary. My parents were amazing through it all, letting me use their car if I paid the insurance and gas. Plus, I could live at home for free, but I needed to always have a job.

It was at GoodLife that I met my now ex-boyfriend. He was nice and made me feel worth something. We started dating. I thought I had to marry this man because both my little brothers, Micheal and Matthew were married to wonderful godly women Jodi and Kayla. They both owned their own homes and held full-time jobs (one even has a son). They had the life I thought I should have. Since I'm the oldest, I had thought that meant first married, first house, first everything. But God broke me of that idealism when they married first.

After nearly two years in my relationship, I suddenly woke up to *"a person I didn't recognize;"* to a pull so strong I thought I would tear in two. I wanted to be in his world—the secular one, and remain in my family's world—the spiritual one. But as I pushed to remain in both, I felt a heaviness I had never known—a push that was so strong I was thrust back into God's world and told to let go. Letting go of the life that had given me a haven from all the expectations I had for my future was one of the hardest things I had ever done.

I cried for days before the breakup knowing what I had to do. When the relationship flat-lined, I immediately set up a budget to go to Korea and sent it to my Korean sister Junyoung. Two days later, she called with a job offer. I told her I needed to pray. But at that time, I had no idea how to hear God or how to rely on Him. I decided to take a trip to Halifax at the end the first week of March to see my oldest friend Kaleigh. It was as I looked out the window from her apartment that I knew I was going to Korea. It brought me nearly to tears as I realized my dream from so many years ago was in God's plan. There was just one problem—I had applied for my Masters in Creative Writing. I threw down my fleece telling God, *"If I'm accepted I'll stay, but if I'm rejected I go"* (Judges 6:37-38). The next day, I received a rejection email from the Master's program. I never thought I would ever celebrate rejection! I accepted the teaching position in South Korea where I would be living with a Christian family.

At the beginning of writing this chapter, I was asked, *"How have you endured?"* To be frank, I don't feel like I have endured, because I wanted to give up and God gave me a spirit not to ever give up!

A few months ago, I hesitated to say that God gave me *anything* or is in *everything*. I struggled seeing how other Christians could throw everything into His hands, believing fully in His unknown plan. I thought that they were foolish, that they should do the legwork, that they should stop showing off their faith, that they should just be silent.

I have since learned to relinquish control. I can drive, but Jesus needs to navigate, no more detours.

No more running away (1 Corinthians 9:24-27). I'm *going the distance!*

STRATEGIES FOR BUILDING YOUR ENDURANCE

1. I often wondered if God really cared about me. What has God done or is He doing in your life to show that He cares?

_____

_____

_____

_____

2. Why haven't you given up? Think about it, what keeps you moving even when life doesn't feel worth living anymore. Dig deeper: why has that thing or person kept you moving forward?

_____

_____

_____

_____

3. Why does God place challenges in your life? What challenges have helped to strengthen you? All challenges can feel negative in the moment, but once you change your perspective you can understand why you face those challenges.

_____

_____

_____

_____

4. Think about: if you had never been challenged, where do you think you would be now? I believe with my whole heart that if I had never gone through even half of my challenges I wouldn't be sitting in Korea today. I would have chosen the wrong path and be faced with sadness, instead of this God given joy.

----

5. In all the trials in your life, how do you know that God was always there? It could take stepping back for a moment. Remove the magnifying glass on the moment you are in and try looking at the big picture of your life. I promise He was carrying you, walking with you, helping you up, and cheering you on the whole time.

----

6. Will you try to stand on your own or let God show you His omnipotence? If we try to stand on our own, we will be afraid of failure and therefore limit ourselves, but if we have faith the size of a mustard seed we can tell the mountain to move and it will move (Matthew 17:20). What is the mountain in your life? What will you choose?

ABOUT ALYSSA HARRINGTON

 Alyssa Harrington was born and raised in Douglas, just outside of Fredericton. She is twenty-five years old and has obtained two degrees, a B.A. with a major in English and a Concentration in Creative Writing as well as an Advanced TESL Certification, followed by a B.Ed. She's worked with kids for the past six years, starting with working at children's church camps and progressing to the Multicultural Association of Fredericton. Alyssa is currently working in Korea as an English teacher at an English Academy, or as they call it, a Hagwon.

Contact Alyssa:
- Facebook: www.Facebook.com/ChristianWriter1991
- Email: DareToDreamWriting@gmail.com

MOST LIKELY TO SUCCEED?

By B. Jacqueline Jeter

MOST LIKELY TO SUCCEED?

"Endurance is not just the ability to bear a hard thing,
but to turn it into glory."
William Barclay

"Hey fatty." "Wow, you are really black." "You're not smart. They just
needed a token in the advanced class and chose you." "Are those your
grandparents?" "Why are you so tall?" "Why do you talk so fast?" "Is
something wrong with you?"

en·dur·ance
1.the fact or power of enduring an unpleasant or difficult process
or situation without giving way.

I started out expecting to have challenges. My mother was 48 and
my father was 52 when I was born. Babies born now, in the face
of advanced technology to parents this old, are expected to have
learning disabilities, functional disabilities, etc.? *But God.*

 I am the fifth child of awesomely wonderful, enterprising and wise
parents, Rosa Sallie Elizabeth Jeter and Robert Lewis Jeter Sr. They
have both taken their permanent homes in heaven, but not without
pouring a wealth of wisdom and knowledge into their baby girl.

Times of scraped knees, taunting, and carefree days

I grew up during a time when *"what I was"* was called a *tomboy.* For
those not knowing what that is, a tomboy is a girl who behaves in
a manner usually considered boyish. I had 3 main friends, two of
which were boys. We played tackle football, stickball, hide and seek,
freeze tag and all the other games kids from our era used to play.
We rode bikes, climbed trees and jumped in and swam in lakes. My

female friend and I did some of the same things, but we also had our girly activities like beauty shop—where we brushed each other's hair and painted our nails. We also tried out our early Food Network star skills by baking pies and making French fries from potatoes we peeled ourselves. While we did all those things as best friends, the same people were also the source of my initial nightmares and low self-esteem upper cuts. I was ridiculed for liking to read and getting straight A grades. I was called *"black Jack"* by the friend who was literally the color of night. As an extroverted, awkward, chubby kid, I was a prime target. However, I wanted what any kid or even adult wants—friends. I was taunted because my parents were so much older than those of my fellow classmates. I developed resentment with God for giving me to them at such an old age.

Confidence boosters from my cheerleaders- My Parents

I remember coming in from school one day, crying after being called a bookworm and teacher's pet. My mother hugged me with one of those hugs that had the capability to bring world peace. She simply said to me *"You just have to be who God made you."* At nine years old, I didn't really want to hear that. When my daddy came home, I shared with him the same story. His response was *"Those that pick at you today will work for you tomorrow."* Again, I'm nine so you can just imagine the look on my face after that one.

I went to bed later and lay there thinking about their words. Tomorrow was going to be a different day. I was going to focus on being just me: a charismatic, science loving, straight A nerd who loves to read and laugh. This will get better right? Well, maybe not so fast.

New Focus. New Opportunities. New Upper Cuts.

One morning I woke up to my mother praying over me. She

apparently did that often, but I was normally sound asleep. Although she said a lot of words, the scripture from Philippians 4:13 NIV *"I can do all things through Him Who gives me strength"* became my focus scripture. I took that to heart and refocused for a ride that I knew would still be difficult, yet I had HIM so nothing else mattered.

As I progressed in school, I had the blessed opportunity to have a guidance counselor who recognized my love for science. She introduced me to summer science camp. By the grace of God and lots of sacrifice from my parents, I spent most of my summers in Boone, NC with like-minded friends. It was like my own special caucus of nerds. Of course, this new opportunity brought new upper cuts from those not as appreciative of my uniqueness as I had become. However, instead of derailing me, it fueled me. I developed my life mantra of *"Keep Pressing"* at the age of 15. My closest friends were now trophies from oratorical contests, academic bowl contests and science fairs. While my parents were still my cheerleaders, I gained more confidence from each jab and from the praises of people with no faces. These people loved my achievements and drive, but did not know the inner Jackie. I was lonely, but now I had others depending on me so I had to *"Keep Pressing."*

In high school, I diversified by adding sports to my life resume. I found that, while I was not being scouted by coaches, I loved the feeling of being part of a team. Basketball, track and cheerleading (chubby kid no more) were new outlets of acceptance. Wow, it worked! I made lifelong friends, some of whom I am still close to today. Of course, new upper cuts came with that. Those, who thought because of the hue of my wrapper I should be eating lunch and hanging with them, took issue with my melanin- challenged confidants. Oh well, I wasn't fazed because now I had real friends who entered the ring with me and threw some upper cuts in the direction of my accusers.

"Keep Pressing!" I can do all things through Him Who gives me strength.

High school was not so bad after all. Before standing on the stage and giving a speech to my graduating class, I added many more achievements to my list. Some of those which shaped who I am today were Student Body President, Governor's School Delegate (another nerd meetup) and the senior class superlative *"Most Likely to Succeed."*

Adulting Before the Term

College years truly tested my mantra. Having matriculated at what I think is the best university in the land (NC State University—home of the Wolfpack) taught me that the distant taunts and jabs from my early years were just preparation. No one really knew me there. I was a minnow in a vast ocean. *"Keep Pressing"* became my breathed prayer during each class. Oddly, there were still those familiar whispers from the peanut gallery, but I had thicker skin now and didn't care. I had to give my parents a return on their investment.

The early seeds of insecurities sown, that I thought I had killed with my success, began to poke through the cracks in my cemented exterior. I lost my election run as Student Government Student Attorney General. That was a blow because I can't remember losing. It was during these *"best years of your life"* that my lead cheerleader, my beautiful mother, laid down her pom-poms and picked up her wings. *"Keep Pressing?"* I wanted to die with her. I still had my dad but there is nothing like a mother's love, especially to a young woman entering her 20s. My strength to press waned. Bad choices ensued, grades dropped, depression knocked on my door and I let her in. It was during this time that the closet skeleton of resentment that I previously had with God appeared with some remaining meat on it. I grew angry that He would take my mother when I needed her most. I grew angry that He would allow a woman who loved Him and exhibited His character effortlessly to suffer from nasty painful cancer. My best friend, Rhea, was an amazing support as well as her mother who had also become mine. However, there is nothing like needing your original incubator.

"Keep Pressing?" Yeah right!

Recalibration Needed

One day while visiting and watching a game with my dad, he said to me *"You need to grow up and be the woman your mother taught you to be. We sacrificed too much for you not to live."* There was a cartoon character named Popeye. He was a sailor with big muscles. His nemesis was named Bluto. Whenever Popeye was in a tight situation or losing strength, he would eat spinach that seemed to give him supernatural strength. I call that talk with my dad: *"The Popeye Talk."* My mission was recalibrated and my strength returned. He left me with the scripture from Proverbs 3:5-6 NIV: *"Trust in the LORD with all your heart, and lean not on your own understanding. In all your ways submit to him, and he will make your paths straight."*

Navigating the Waters

The voice of my co-President of my Cheerleading Council was silenced and he joined my mother in the heavenly stands. All the talks and droplets of wisdom they imparted into me began to make sense. Whenever anything came up, I went to the playbook they gave me—the Word of God. I can hear my mother saying, *"Keep your eyes on God, Baby"* or my dad telling me *"You have to endure some hard things in life, but it is not the end."* My resentment for God giving me older parents turned to thanksgiving. My other friends did not have these wisdom pearls that I had.

I've applied those pearls, which really is the Word of God, to my life. I've had a beautiful life of success in my career as a scientist and in my relationships with my siblings and friends. It has definitely not been easy but, with my eyes fixed on Jesus, it has been bearable. My faith has been enriched by the challenges. Occasionally, I sank in the water like Peter, but when I refocused I was able to walk on the sea again.

"Keep Pressing?" YES!

The Word of God tells us in James 1:2-4 NIV: *"Consider it pure joy, my brothers and sisters, whenever you face trials of many kinds, because you know that the testing of your faith produces perseverance. Let perseverance finish its work so that you may be mature and complete, not lacking anything."*

I've seen this word grow legs in my life. I have it posted on one of my mirrors so that I am reminded that, when I want to quit, I must endure. There is someone depending on me and someone depending on you. Like a cake baking in the oven, you have to wait till the process is complete so you can partake of the sweetness thereof. You have to endure seeing the ingredients mixed together. You have to endure the tantalizing smell of it baking in the oven. You have to endure the cooling process once it is taken out of the oven. Through all of that, you don't just throw up your hands and say forget it. No, you endure until it goes through all the steps before you can savor every morsel.

Similarly, you have to endure the process of life, so that you can be that sweet smelling savor to the Lord and to those who He has assigned to your life.

I believe that our life is like a patchwork quilt. All of the things we go through make up the beauty of that quilt. If you quit or acquiesce from a challenge by not enduring, you will have a missing patch in the quilt and it will never be able to bring the full beauty and warmth for which it was designed.

My focus is to please Him. In high school, it was to please people. I still want to be Most Likely to Succeed, but instead of pursuing achievements I'm pursuing Him. My new superlative is to hear from Him the words of Matthew 25:21 *"Well done, good and faithful servant! You have been faithful with a few things; I will put you in charge of many things. Come and share your master's happiness!"*

ENDURE! *"Keep Pressing!"* Your life and the lives of others depend on it!

"Don't give up. Don't ever give up." Jim Valvano

STRATEGIES FOR BUILDING YOUR ENDURANCE

1. Romans 8:28 states *"And we know that in all things God works for the good of those who love Him, who have been called according to His purpose."* What are three things happening in your life right now to which you can apply this verse to buttress your strength to endure?

---

2. Our circumstances can at times be very overwhelming and cause us to faint or lose the drive to keep pressing. What things have you learned or put in place to help you to endure a negative or unpleasant situation? What scriptures give you strength to endure?

_____

_____

_____

_____

3. Proverbs 3:5-6 *"Trust in the LORD with all your heart and lean not on your own understanding; in all your ways submit to Him, and He will make your paths straight."* In what areas do you need to recalibrate your relationship with God and trust Him more?

_____

_____

_____

_____

4. It has been said that you cannot conquer what you won't confront. List circumstances in your life that you need to confront and conquer. Identify which and where these circumstances thwarted your growth to move forward.

_____

_____

_____

_____

5. Identify those persons in your life who have:

caused you not to endure:

_____

_____

_____

_____

encouraged you to endure:

_____

_____

_____

_____

ABOUT B. JACQUELINE JETER

Lover of the Lover of her soul! Teacher of God's word. Encourager! Intercessor! These are just a few words to describe B. Jacqueline Jeter, a woman after the heart of God. She has a passion for God and His people, especially youth, to help them to be empowered to realize their full potential naturally and spiritually.

Jacqueline is a an experienced clinical development project leader, licensed Minister and a faithful participant of Bible Study Fellowship (BSF) International for 15 years where she served as group leader for 5 years. Most notably, she is an Independent Certified Coach, Teacher and Speaker with The John Maxwell Team.

Jacqueline has been blessed to travel the world, setting foot on every continent except for Africa and Antarctica. She believes that the Lord uses her to minister to persons and to pray for the lands where she travels. Her favorite verse is 2 Corinthians 2:14 (NLT) *"But thank God! He has made us his captives and continues to lead us along in Christ's triumphal procession. Now he uses us to spread the knowledge of Christ everywhere, like a sweet perfume."*

She is the visionary of an encouragement blog, *ReignDrops* and the CEO of the soon to be launched business, *The Ripple Effect Development Group*.

Contact Jacqueline:
- Website: www.HisReignDrops.com
- Facebook: www.Facebook.com/Reign-Drops-902446183125067
- Twitter: www.Twitter.com/ReignDropsBJJ
- Email: HisReignDrops@gmail.com
- Phone: 919-453-6337

ENDURANCE PRECEDES ADVERSITY

By Tiffany Johnson

ENDURANCE PRECEDES ADVERSITY

"The LORD is my rock, my fortress, and my savior; my God is my rock in Whom I find protection. He is my shield, the strength of my salvation, and my stronghold."
Psalm 18:2 NLT

It was 4 o'clock in the morning, but I couldn't sleep. I was sitting there in a hospital bed, waiting for the nurse to bring in the next round of pain medicine. Although the pain I was in was very intense at times, my inability to sleep was more from God prompting me, yet again, to spend time with Him. I opened up my devotional book and saw the scripture referenced of Psalm 18:2. Tears started streaming down my cheeks as I read that verse and looked up the rest of the chapter. I sobbed out loud as I thought about my LORD, my Savior Who was my Shield and Protection when, only two days earlier, I had endured the most horrific accident I could have imagined—a shark attack.

I was enjoying the colorful fish and coral reef as I floated there breathing through my snorkel mask in the clear Bahama waters. It was beautiful and something I enjoyed seeing year after year as my husband and I traveled to different places in the Caribbean. Our love for snorkeling was birthed out of our time in Maui on our honeymoon and has been something we've enjoyed doing together ever since then.

I was alone in the water at that time. My husband went back to the boat with an upset stomach and things to take care of, if you know what I mean. So I stayed in the water because after all, twenty minutes is not enough time to take in God's underwater creation. I was floating there just taking in the views, when I felt a sensation of bumping into something—almost like a small tug on my arm. As I casually turned to see what I had bumped into, my eyes locked on to these small black beady eyes and I began to realize what was taking place. I was face to face with a shark and my entire arm was clenched in his jaws. I felt my eyes get big as reality set in. Time stood still for a moment as I floated there staring at this shark who had my arm pinned. He didn't make any violent movements; he just floated there staring at me, almost as if he was saying, *"Your move."*

"The grave wrapped its ropes around me; death itself
stared me in the face."
Psalm 18:5 NLT

Then, all at once, time caught up with us and I yanked my arm back, trying to break free from his grip. It was game on for him as he began to thrash and fight me. In that moment, the strength of the Lord rose up from within me allowing me to fight! I don't know how many times I tried yanking my arm from his clenched teeth, as the thoughts rushed through my mind, *"You are not going to take my life! I am not going to die here."* Then I yanked again and his jaws opened. In pulling out what was left of my arm, I saw only a mangled stump. My hand and lower arm was completely gone. Flipping to my left side, I threw off my snorkel mask and cried out, *"Help me! Help me Jesus!"*

"But in my distress I cried out to the Lord; yes,
I prayed to my God for help.
He heard me from His sanctuary; my cry reached His ears."
Psalm 18:6

Furiously, I began to swim back to the boat, raising my wounded arm above the water. I prayed in the Holy Spirit and cried out, *"Help me Jesus"* with each stroke towards the boat. Blood was spraying out of what was left of my arm, leaving a substantial blood trail in the water surrounding me. I looked up to see sheer terror in my husband's eyes, as he looked in disbelief at the scene before him.

It was something you would see in a scary movie. But without hesitation, he jumped into the water and began to make his way towards me. As he helped me into the boat, I felt the peace of the Lord so strongly—it was a thick, tangible cloud surrounding me. I calmly instructed him to get a beach towel, tie it as tight as possible, and to elevate my arm. Laying my head in his lap, I closed my eyes and immediately began to pray again.

"He reached down from heaven and rescued me; He drew me out of deep waters.
He delivered me from my powerful enemies, from those who hated me and were too strong for me.
They attacked me at a moment when I was weakest, but the LORD upheld me. He led me to a place of safety; He rescued me because He delights in me."
Psalm 18:16-19 NLT

So there I was, two days later, sitting in my hospital bed at four o'clock in the morning, reading the description of my own testimony through Psalm 18! I wept, thinking about the love God has for me and how He rescued me and gave me a second chance. In those days following the attack, I had a choice to make. I could easily play the victim role, blame God, shut myself off from everyone, and ask, *"Why me?"* OR, I could proclaim that God is good no matter what (Nahum 1:7), that He is my peace and my strength (Psalm 29:11) and that He has the best in mind for me (Jeremiah 29:11).

I chose the latter, because how could I not give God the glory for saving my life? It doesn't make sense why the shark LET me swim away from him, or why he didn't drown me in the first place. On top of that, I was breathing through my snorkel tube during the entire attack. That means my snorkel tube (sticking out only a mere 2-3 inches above water) never left the surface, because I never swallowed any sea water amidst the struggle. The shark amputated my arm and all I had was a beach towel (no tourniquet) to stop the bleeding for a 30 minute boat ride back to the port, yet I didn't lose enough blood to require a blood transfusion, I didn't lose consciousness, and I never fought infection! These are miracles that cannot be explained in any other way but God's intervention.

My testimony shows how *endurance* is possible in the face of tragedy, the unknown, the problems, the problems, the everyday slumps, the depression...the list could go on and on. However, *endurance* itself is not something that appears or develops overnight. It's not something you can just muster up on your own. No, *true endurance* comes from what you choose to put inside of you every single day.

The Word of God equips us and is our training manual on life (2 Timothy 3:16-17). The more we are filled with God's Word, the more we will instinctively turn to it and claim the promises He has for us when faced with problems, big or small. If you don't know His promises and don't hide His word in your heart (Psalm 119:11), how will you stand when adversity comes? How will you endure? What you put in comes out eventually, and when the fire comes, you will find out quickly who and what your hope and trust really relies on.

If you aren't there yet, if you haven't made a relationship with Jesus a priority—it's not too late! Friend, I urge you to pick up your Bible, download the free bible app, use google to search scriptures or whatever you need to do to read God's Word. Make a daily habit of reading it and spending time in prayer.

It really should be no different than the close relationships we have with our friends or family. We need to talk to and listen to them, learn about them and spend time with them in order to grow and maintain a close relationship. Our relationship with God is the same. We need to talk with Him openly and listen to what He is saying through our prayer time. We need to learn about His character, Who He is, and how we can deepen our relationship with Him through reading His Word. And we need to spend time with Him by worshipping Him and proclaiming Who He is in our lives.

In the two weeks preceding this horrendous attack, I woke up several times early in the morning before my husband and kids got up. I felt this strong urge to pray and have my devotion time. I bartered with God telling Him that, if I was still awake a half hour later, I would get up. Sure enough, a half hour later I was still awake. So I was obedient (reluctant at first, I might add) and God met me there in those days prior to the attack. I even woke up a few different times on the cruise itself before my husband got up, and just spent time with Jesus. Truthfully, I had been lacking in my personal time with Him.

I made excuses like *"I work full time," "I have too much to do around the house," "I am too busy taking care of my three very young children, so I am exhausted and just don't have time."* God gave me the time, because He knew what I needed! He knew what I was about to endure.

Being the good Daddy He is, He knew I needed a little bit extra—a fresh encounter with Him—to get through what He knew was coming. It reminds me of how God prepared Jesus for the cross at the garden of Gethsemane. Jesus stayed up all through the night praying and seeking God right before He was crucified. *God was giving Jesus exactly what He needed to endure* that horrific experience. Similarly, God was preparing me too!

Though those handful of mornings spent with Jesus before the attack have helped me to proclaim that the joy of the Lord is my strength (Nehemiah 8:10), in the aftermath of it, they are not solely responsible. Being able to truly proclaim the joy of the Lord is my strength largely results from a lifestyle change I had made years ago, when I set the intention of following Jesus and strive to be more like Him.

The word *ENDURANCE* signifies something long-lasting—something strong, persistent, and unwavering. I believe *the secret to true endurance* is the only One Who is always strong, persistent, and unwavering. My trust is not built on things of this world; it is solely on God (Proverbs 3:5-6). I, myself, am weak and mess up, but His grace is sufficient in my weakness (2 Corinthians 12:9).

I am also facing a new struggle of doing life with only one hand. I have discovered over these past two months that some simple everyday tasks have become impossible for me to do single-handed. I can't put my hair up in a ponytail when I am having a bad hair day, tie my own shoes or put on my favorite pair of diamond stud earrings. In these moments I have gotten frustrated, been short with my husband and have fought back thoughts of defeat. It is also in these moments where I have to take those thoughts captive (2 Corinthians 10:5), proclaim God's goodness no matter what, and trust God in all things. It is a *choice to endure*, not something that just happens. It is a choice I have to make every day.

I still have a long road of recovery and a lot to endure ahead of me, but the most vital thing I have learned about *endurance* is that it *precedes adversity.* When trials come, when we are walking through a tragedy, or when we are facing those everyday struggles, *the substance of our endurance comes from how we are satisfying that void and longing in our lives.* If that void is being filled with God's Word and our relationship with Him, then we can stand on the promises He has for us no matter the circumstance.

One scripture I will leave with you...that I have stood on during this time and will continue to stand on is James 1:2-4 (NLT):

"Dear brothers and sisters,
*whenever **trouble** comes your way,*
*let it be an **opportunity for joy**.*
*For when your **faith is tested**,*
*your **endurance** has a chance to grow.*
So let it grow,
for when your endurance is fully developed,
*you will be **strong in character** and **ready for anything**."*

STRATEGIES FOR BUILDING YOUR ENDURANCE

1.Take a moment to think of a time when God showed up and pulled you through. What past storm, challenge, or trial have you overcome because of Jesus? It changes our perspective when we remember what God has done! (Psalm 77:11-12)

_____

_____

_____

_____

2.What is holding you back from fully trusting in God?

_____

_____

_____

_____

3. What steps will you take to build on your relationship with God?

_____

_____

_____

_____

Prayer: *Lord Jesus, please forgive me for any time where I have not fully trusted in You. I know You have the best in mind for me. Help me to see that even when the storms of life come, You are always there with me to strengthen and help me overcome (Isaiah 41:10). I pray that you would spark in me a fire that cannot be put out! Help me to be diligent in spending time in Your Word, prayer, and worship. I pray for less of me and more of You so that when people see me, they see Jesus! Amen*

ABOUT TIFFANY JOHNSON

Tiffany Johnson is a recent shark attack survivor who has chosen to trust God in all things. She is an author, worship leader and speaker, but most importantly a daughter of the King of Kings. Her and her husband, James, were college pastors for four years and now reside in North Carolina with their three children. Both Tiffany and her Husband are very active in their church, The Refuge in Kannapolis, NC. Tiffany has recently been speaking at numerous churches sharing her testimony of faith, miracles and enduring through her tragedy. You can connect with Tiffany via her Facebook page, *Tiffany Johnson: Trusting God In All Things.*

Contact Tiffany:
- Facebook: www.Facebook.com/BAnOvercomer

RUNNING THE RACE... AND FINISHING

By Dennis LaRue Jr.

RUNNING THE RACE...AND FINISHING

When I think about endurance, I return to the days when I was a long-distance runner. Like Forrest Gump proudly said I can proudly say, *"I could run like the wind blows."* To my family and friends, they probably thought about me like the men sitting in town thought about a young Forrest running by, saying he was *"a running fool."* I remember literally running wherever I needed to go. I ran to work 6 miles away. I often ran to my best friend's house during the summer, a four-mile one-way trip, because his mom's cupcakes were to die for.

I look back on those days of running fast and free with the wind blowing through my hair. I can still feel the breeze cooling my body all drenched in sweat. I ran in the extreme heat and in the ice and snow. I ran like a deer, effortless, bouncing along. I can remember thinking about how much I enjoyed every step. I could effortlessly run 10 and 12 miles while talking with my teammates every step of the way. I was 16. At this time of my life, perseverance was the furthest thing from my mind because I was good at everything I did: running, school, even work. I felt invincible. I was on top of the world. I was the King of Me–ville with a population of one...ME!

One of my first endurance tests occurred during my freshman year of college. I was running faster and farther than ever. I was named to the Freshman All-Region cross-country team and was setting personal best times on the track. Unfortunately, I was not setting personal best scores academically. I was not running to class as I should have but was running from class instead. My grades were so bad that if my Grade Point Average (GPA) was compared to an Earned Run Average (ERA) for a professional baseball pitcher, I would have won the best pitcher of the year! I was academically ineligible to compete as a runner. I was depressed, angry and felt like an utter failure. This is the first time I really felt like a failure. My running endurance was at its prime but my life endurance muscles were just getting started.

I swallowed my wounded pride and moved back home, found a job, and transferred to junior college. It was during this time when I met my wife. God used her as an instrument to bring me to Himself on April 30th, 1991. That night, I turned over the keys to Me-ville and became a member of the God's Kingdom. I was forever changed and I discovered that my endurance would be tested daily from here on out.

The Christian life is often compared with a marathon. I agree with this comparison because as a runner there is a big difference between a 100-meter sprint and 26.2 miles. I dare you to run a 100-meter sprint as fast as you can. Not much of a dare, is it? Ok, I double-dog dare you to run a 26.2-mile marathon as fast as you possibly can from the starting line all the way to the finish line. How's that for a dare? Are you likely to cross the finish line—alive? Of course not. You are likely to receive what the running community calls a DNF (Did Not Finish), a title no runner (especially me) wants to see next to his name in post-racing results.

The Christian life is like running a marathon. Many of us start out *"on fire for the Lord"* with a passion that consumes everyone and everything on our path. We are bold in sharing our new-found faith to the point of being perceived as rude, uncaring and pushy. We read our Bibles with a hunger to learn that, if we read like that during our high school or formative education years, we might have been given Ivy League scholarships. We attended every church function and service with an excitement where we were the first to arrive and the last to leave. There is an overwhelming feeling of excitement, freedom, joy and gratitude. This was what I experienced when I started my faith journey. I believe I am not alone.

The problem for runners isn't starting the marathon race—it's finishing. I believe the problem finishing exists within the Christian community. Many start the race but not everyone finishes the race. Why? I believe the Apostle Paul's words to the church at Corinth instruct us about running the race of faith. He said, *"Do you not know that those who run in a race all run, but one receives the prize? Run in such a way that you may obtain it"* (1 Corinthians 9:24, NKJV). To run in such a way to win the prize requires intense training, discipline, consistency and a mindsight focused not on quitting, but focused on winning.

This same mindset exists in Olympic athletes like Steve *"Pre"* Prefontaine. Pre was and still is revered in the running community as America's greatest distance runner. He was known for his ferocious racing style, his disciplined training regime, and his intense desire to win. He exemplified the mindset of winning when he was cited in *The Quotable Runner* saying, *"A lot of people run a race to see who's the fastest. I run to see who has the most guts."* What Pre said is important because you can't win without *endurance*. We do not *just* have *"guts"*—we develop them. A journey of faith requires that we develop guts. Winning the prize requires guts. Everyone wants to experience the joy of winning a race, however very few are willing to pay the price required to receive the prize.

Dear friend, what price are you willing to pay to finish your journey to the finish line? How will you do it?

I shared with you earlier that I've been running since I was a kid. Yet, I did not run my first marathon until I was 37 years old! That's a long time to be a seasoned competitive runner and not run a marathon. Why did it take me so long to run a marathon? Honestly, I was afraid. That's right, a competitive distance runner afraid of distance running. I was terrified of experiencing what marathon runners call *"hitting the wall."*

The famous *"Wall"* is where your body has completely exhausted all forms of fuel in the body. Your muscles start locking up. Your arms and legs feel like cement weights. You feel almost out of control of your body. You feel as if you are moving in super slow motion. These phenomena can happen almost without warning. One minute a runner feels as if they are gliding along like a deer in a field, running effortlessly, enjoying the moment, and the other runners, then BOOM—the wheels come off, the glide becomes a slow jog, a walk or even a crawl. Most marathoners experience the *"Wall"* right around the 20-miler marker. If you are doing the math, that's 6.2 miles left to go to reach the finish line with little to no fuel. Hitting the *"wall"* tests every runner's physical, mental and emotional endurance.

The journey of life is no different than the marathon. You will hit at least one, if not many *"Walls"* during your life's race. It's not a matter of *"if"*—it's a matter of *"when"*. Your *physical, mental and emotional endurance* will be (if it hasn't already been) tested. Are you prepared to endure the *"Walls"* impact to your job or career? What about in your home, within your marriage or family? When the *"Wall"* comes knocking on the door of your health, will you stand? What about your finances? The *"Wall"* will even show up in the form of your closest relationships like your BFF's.

Your faith will be tested with each *"Wall"* when it appears. You will face many of these *"Walls"*—I promise you this. What I can also promise you is that you can endure them to the end and cross the finish line running on all cylinders rather than a death crawl!

You probably wondering, how do I overcome the *"Walls"* of life?

There are some days when you won't feel like getting out of bed. You'll be tired, grumpy or even anxious. What I want to share with you are the lessons I learned that helped me cross the finish line of my marathons that I also applied in my life to help me overcome many of life's *"Walls."* I believe these lessons, when applied, will help you endure and overcome the obstacles in your life.

The AHA Moment–Your Why Means Everything!

Do you want to know how I finally conquered my fear or the marathon?

It wasn't because of lengthy conversations with seasoned marathon runners or books on the subject. Frankly, I'm embarrassed to tell you. I finally conquered my fear of the marathon after reading an old celebrity article from *Runner's World* magazine about Oprah Winfrey. Oprah trained for and completed the Marine Corp Marathon in Washington, D.C. The great Oprah Winfrey ran a marathon! Oprah was not a lifelong distance runner like me— far from it! Yet, she completed more marathons than this lifelong runner. Oprah was ahead 1-0. I remember saying to myself, *"If Oprah can run a marathon and finish it, so can I."* That was my marathon *"AHA"* moment.

AHAs are moments of clarity, raising your personal level of awareness in your mind like a flash of light instantly shining a dark room. AHAs power your mind and heart which leads you toward taking a desired action. The AHA is where you discover your *"WHY."*

In his book *Start With Why*, author Simon Sinek describes your why as *"the purpose, reason or cause for what it is you are doing."* Granted my why was based on competing with Oprah at the time, but I also was challenging myself to do what I had never done before and I had to conquer my fear. Oprah helped me to see that I could indeed run and complete a marathon. My entire perception of the marathon changed. My thoughts went from fear of the *"Wall"* to instant belief that I could do it.

What *"Wall"* are you facing right now? Maybe your marriage is suffering? Maybe you have received a medical diagnosis you were not expecting. Whatever your challenge is, you must discover your reason why for overcoming it. Your Why is the fuel for overcoming all obstacles. If your Why is strong enough, you will break through any *"Wall"* standing in your path.

Feed Your Faith and Starve Your Fear

Once I had my AHA moment, I had this sudden sense of possibility. I can run a marathon. I felt the energy of that thought. I heard the words coming from my mouth. I felt turbo-charged and ready to go. After a good night's rest, my fears showed back up in full force reminding me of the terror of the *"Wall."* My fears were coming back stronger than before.

Do you know what I did to quiet my fears?

I felt the fear, went online, registered, and paid for my marathon. No turning back now. I fed my belief that I could do it by signing up and committing to get into the race. I also saw myself crossing the finish line every time I trained. I envisioned *FINISHING* the race!

When you are hearing the doubts and fears whispering their lies into your ears, you need to shut them down with your faith! The Bible describes *faith* as *"the substance of things hoped for, the evidence of things not seen"* (Hebrews 11:1, NKJV). What are you *hoping* for?

Think about what you are hoping for, then *speak* what you are hoping for *TO your fears*. Remember your *Why*, then add to it *the faith* that you *will* overcome your *"Wall."* *Act* now by writing out positive verses, quotes and affirmations that will fuel your faith. *Record* a positive word from those who mean the most to you. Today, to fuel my faith as a transformational change agent, I have index cards with quotes from speeches that inspire me. I wrote these quotes out as if the speaker said them only to me. Then, I the speaker sign the quote to affirm their quote was just for me. I read them 3-4 times a day as reminder to feed my faith and starve my fear.

Get Your Support Team Together

I may have run the marathon by myself, but I didn't get to the starting line or the finish line by myself. I had a support team consisting of a partner to train me, a coach to advise me and (the most important part of my team) a cheering section to encourage me onward!

My training partner was also like a coach to me. He was an experienced marathoner, running more marathons than I could count. He and I met 5 days a week to train at 5:15 AM. By committing to run with him, I was held accountable. Coaches hold their clients (runners) accountable. I saw mine at work every single day. If I missed a workout, he just gave me the look—that said it all! He challenged and encouraged me to overcome obstacles. You need to have a training partner. Find someone who will hold you accountable, who will encourage you, and who will pray with you and for you. Have as many as you need. For me as a runner, all I needed was a single partner. But, committed in my life to being a great leader and coach, I have several training partners when it comes to growing my faith.

The Final Lap To The Finish Line

Athletes love to feel the energy of their home crowd. As a runner, I love the hearing my name shouted from the crowd, especially when I am hitting the physical, mental and emotional exhaustion caused by the *"Wall."* My family was my cheering section for my marathon. I can remember seeing them at the finish line. I felt a sudden burst of energy to finish as strong as possible. That's the power a cheering section can have on you. You need to have the same type of people on your support team who will applaud you, cheer you up and sometimes carry you when you need a hand. The *"Wall"* takes no prisoners. Neither will you.

Some of you have not yet reached any of these *"Walls."* That's good because the time to prepare for them is now before you hit one. Some of you have made it through a *"Wall"*—Congratulations! Help those who are going through *"Walls"* by being a member of their support team. Help them through *"what you went through."* Some of you are going through a *"Wall"* right now. Don't give up. You are stronger than you think. *"But he who endures to the end shall be saved"* (Matthew 24:13, NKJV).

I no longer fear the marathon or the once dreaded *"Wall."* I still face obstacles in my life. But, when I remember my AHA/WHY, feed my faith and starve my fear, and access my valuable support team, I know that, while obstacles in front of me may look like mountains, I will eventually overcome them. Like me, you too will endure, defeat your *"Walls,"* and finish your race!

STRATEGIES FOR BUILDING YOUR ENDURANCE

1. What is happening in your life right now where you are thinking about taking a DNF – Did Not Finish?

_____

_____

_____

2. What fears are keeping you from running your race?

_____

_____

_____

_____

3. I feared hitting the *"Wall"* but I faced my fear, hit the wall and finished the race. What wall do you need to overcome in your life?

_____

_____

_____

_____

4. Why are you doing what you are doing? Have you found your purpose?

_____

_____

_____

_____

5. Who do you need to add to your support team? Write them down and contact each of them today.

_____

_____

_____

_____

6. What price are you willing to pay to finish your journey to the finish line?

_____

_____

_____

_____

ABOUT DENNIS LARUE JR.

Dennis is an International Transformational Change Agent...personally, professionally and globally who founded LDR – Leaders Develop Relationships to change the world. Dennis believes that all problems, no matter how complex they seem, can be broken down to fundamental solutions. As an international coach, he was part of the transformation of Paraguay, South America. He is an outstanding coach who connects with you to hold you accountable, will challenge your thinking and encourages you to reach your next level...leading to results.

He retired from the United States Air Force in 2015 after a distinguished 23-year career. He served in various leadership roles as a management consultant, program manager, public speaker and trainer. He still serves the military community facilitating *Total Force Leadership Development Program* workshops at Joint Base San Antonio military installations.

Dennis is an internationally certified Executive Coach, Keynote Speaker and Trainer by the #1 Coaching company in the world, the John Maxwell Team. He serves as an Executive Director and Presidential Advisory Council member. Dennis applies John Maxwell's timeless leadership principles, blends them with the wisdom gained from a lifetime of service as a husband, father, grandfather, pastor and military professional to add value to your organization.

He is married to his best friend, Jamie LaRue, has three amazing grown children and two precious grandchildren.

Contact Dennis:
- Website: www.JohnMaxwellGroup.com/DennisLaRue
- LinkedIn: www.LinkedIn.com/in/Dennis-Larue-Jr
- Facebook: www.Facebook.com/DennisLaRueJrLLC
- Twitter: www.Twitter.com/DennisLaRue
- Email: Dennis.LaRueJr@gmail.com

IT'S THE MIDDLE MILE AGAIN
By Ruth E. Meed, BA, MAT, MS

IT'S THE MIDDLE MILE AGAIN

"Therefore do not cast away your confidence,
which has great recompense of reward.
For you have need of patience,
so that after you have done the will of God
you might receive the promise."
Hebrews 10:35-36

I keenly remember the unusual extreme anxiety that gripped my chest. The unexplained pain in my back would not ease. The desperately itchy rash covering my body had not subsided with the doctor recommended medications. I was alone, pacing my house, praying, with no answers to handle the pain and itching. As I did, a sudden shock wave of electricity started to burn its way from my neck down through my left arm causing it to curl and stiffen up until I could not move it anymore. This searing sizzle continued down my left side to my leg which then also curled up, then across to the right leg which instantly froze. I collapsed into a chair because I could no longer move and all my muscles were tightening up to complete rigidity. I had just three fingers of my right hand still moving and I used them to dial 911. This began the story of the last seven years. I was getting no answers from the medical professionals. Two days later the paralysis happened again, this time my entire body froze for 20 minutes. I was conscious, but unable to move. Doctors varied from saying something was very seriously wrong with me to telling me I had a self-created mental problem. I had no answers, I had no hope medically. I was getting weaker and sicker and helplessly wondered if I was dying. I had to hope in God or give up and die.

I languished on the couch that next Sunday unable to do much of anything, let alone attend church. I turned on the radio to listen to a local church broadcast. The preacher said, *"Today we're going to talk about storms and how you can handle that storm, so let's look at the life of Peter and his walk on the water."* (Matthew 14:23-34) He spent the next thirty minutes talking about trusting God and how sometimes God puts us in a *"boat"* and sends us into the middle of a storm to show Himself strong. He also pointed out that even when we fail to trust Jesus, sinking like Peter, He still reaches out to help us the minute we ask Him. I felt in that moment like God in His kindness had reached down to personally encourage me.

When that broadcast finished, another service came on. This next pastor said, *"Folks, I want you to turn in your Bibles to the passage in the New Testament about the storm on the Sea of Galilee and today we will discuss how we deal with storms by looking at Peter's walk on the water."* I nearly gasped aloud realizing that my Loving Shepherd had providentially orchestrated both of those messages, one right after the other to encourage me to trust Him when I had no answers.

After lunch, I listened to the morning service from my church. My pastor was reviewing what he had covered so far in Isaiah. He repeatedly rehearsed the theme of Isaiah *"Trust ye in the Holy One of Israel alone, for He only is salvation."* He related this concept to how we deal with troubles in our lives. *"We can be distressed. Life can be full of questions and hard things, but we can always trust the hand of our Loving Father to guide us THROUGH them."* I lay there basking in the feeling of those healing Words washing over my soul. Through these three messages from three different sources over four hours' time, the almost palpable hug from God assuring me He was walking with me could not be mistaken. My Loving Lord in His Sovereignty had orchestrated that day's programing to tell me that I could trust Him in this storm.

That was August 2010. By January 2011, I could no longer walk or balance myself. I could not think straight to read or write. Something was very wrong. The doctor told me there was nothing more she could do and to pray that my body would get better. I was a professor at a university and needed to keep working, but was utterly weak and dizzy most days and had now lost an unexplained 70 pounds. Finally, after 7 months recovering, I started teaching 1-2 hours a day again. This slow process to regain strength and balance and concentration enough to just do the basics of teaching was accomplished only in God's strength, one day, or sometimes, just one hour at a time. In the coming months and years there would be many times when I would ask myself, *"Where was God in all this? Was God still good? Did He still love me? Was He still in control and could I trust him? Was I all done ministering for Him? Was I dying? What had I done wrong that I was in this position?"* Those very real questions have warred in my mind through these last seven years. My body never did fully recover and I have battled constant dizziness, extreme fatigue, weakness and unpredictable health since then. Even as I continued to work, I would daily have to wait for the dizziness to pass before I could get up and get ready for teaching that I loved. Medical misdiagnosis, drug reactions and dealing with withdrawals along with an illness I had contracted as a child all had combined to create this crisis. The story of how I discovered answers and causes in God's time is in another book in process. For now, the focus is on how I learned *ENDURANCE* in these long years of trial.

In the early months of 2011 when all I could do was eat, sleep and wonder if I was dying, God gave me this verse: *"Unto you that fear my name will the Son of Righteousness arise with healing in his wings, and you shall go forth and grow up as calves of the stall"* (Malachi 4:2). Little did I know then how long I would be persevering to see that happen. God had prepared me before to trust Him. He had allowed other trials before this. Cancer claimed my father, whom I adored, when I was 35 years old. A thousand mile trip produced negative results, when I searched for a runaway foster daughter, only to have her choose to walk away into a life of misery after I found her. I, like David, had a dear friend with whom I took sweet counsel in the house of God inexplicably walk away wanting nothing more to do with me. Abuse from several individuals emotionally, sexually, and spiritually made me wonder if life was even worth living. The constant antagonism, screaming and controlling accusations of significant people in my life created great confusion and pain for me. Yet I still chose to say, *"God is good and what He does is good no matter what."* How have I come to this place of enduring trust in God despite these trials? The full answer is a book in itself, but for now, I will detail some basic principles I have learned from God in these days of ongoing trial.

The first principle was the choice to keep truth always before my eyes. In those early months, my prayer board held a card from a dear friend who had endured years of debilitating health issues. It simply said: *"What God does in us while we wait is at least as important as the thing for which we are waiting."* I learned then that I needed to wait on God. Andrew Murray's book *Waiting on God* is filled with rich truths on that kind of *endurance*. My Loving Savior was teaching me *endurance*.

Endurance is what it takes to make a quilt. Endurance is a spider weaving its web each night though it would be destroyed by morning, just doing what needs to be done this moment, and leaving the results to his Creator. Endurance is a mother bird brooding over her eggs until they hatch. Endurance for me was waiting on God when nothing made sense and I felt physically inadequate most of the time.

World-renowned leadership expert, John C. Maxwell, often says, *"A leader is one who knows the way, goes the way and shows the way."* I have learned you cannot be the kind of difference-making person God wants you to be until you have learned *endurance*. You must walk that way before you can show others how to walk there.

"But you have need of endurance that after you have done the will of God, you might receive the promise."
(Hebrews 10:36)

The indignation that burned in my heart when I read that verse about two years into this trial of utter unexplained weakness, debilitating fatigue and brain fog indicated my weariness. In frustration, I blurted out, *"God, I don't want to know how to endure, why do I have to deal with endurance? Have I not put up with enough already?"* I could relate with David in his cry of Psalm 69:1-3 *"Save me, O God; for the waters are come in unto my soul. I sink in deep mire, where there is no standing: I am come into deep waters, where the floods overflow me. I am weary of my crying: my throat is dried: mine eyes fail while I wait for my God."* But despite myself, and because of the enabling power of the Holy Spirit, in the days that followed, I started to pay attention to that word *endurance*, what it meant, and how it applied to me. This was *the second principle*: quietly submitting to what God was teaching me.

The third principle was preparation. How did God prepare me to walk through this fire? It started with being born in Ethiopia, raised in a missionary home, and memorizing Bible verses from the time I could talk and then singing them once I was old enough. The desire to know God grew when, at age seven, I trusted Jesus to be my personal Savior from sin. This relationship continued as I endured the challenging years of adjusting to being a third culture kid in Canada which was to me a *"foreign"* country when we moved back home from Ethiopia in 1975. Needing Jesus to be my source of hope and truth was firmly cemented when I worked for seven years at a group home for abused and neglected girls in New Hampshire. Only God's Word could offer healing comfort for the suffering those girls had experienced.

I learned another principle working there. We had a motto: *"stay strong in the middle mile.*" When you start a marathon, everybody's excited, the adrenaline rush is there and you take off. But in the middle of the marathon, there isn't anybody anymore. There are no cheering crowds, no audience, just you, your God and your desire to finish well! When I attended New Brunswick Bible Institute in the 1980s, our instructor Kenneth M. Robins said, *"Anybody can start well, but, will you end well?"* He often reminded us, *"It's what you do in the middle mile that determines whether you end well."* When nobody is looking, when your body is screaming and everything demands you quit, you must keep going.

You must persevere, you must endure. When you have nothing left, you finally realize that your strength was not yours anyway, it was God all along. In your weakness, He becomes your strength, and anything that is accomplished is only because of His enabling power (2 Corinthians 12:9-10).

Thus, I learned that the Christian Life is walked one day at a time. We run it sometimes and walk it sometimes, and if necessary go back to crawling like babies again sometimes, one day at a time. Regardless of how you begin your life with Christ, what you do in the middle mile determines your finish! My focus on God's Word in the middle mile was not always a deep hour-long process because I was too sick to do so. Sometimes it was only a phrase or two at a time that I could understand and cling to. I would read the Psalms or different Bible reading plans as I could to absorb truth. More importantly, I learned the power of sharing those simple truths He was teaching me with other people. I took God's exhortation literally, in Hebrews 3:13 *"to exhort one another daily."* And in the months following my initial illness, I started a habit of sharing my daily verses with others who asked for them. I discovered it not only helped the other person, it helped me! I was kept accountable to the Word as I shared what He was teaching me and I became His channel of blessing in the lives of others. Hebrews 10:23-25 says, *"Let us hold fast the profession of our faith without wavering; for He is faithful that promised; And let us consider one another to provoke unto love and to good works: ...exhorting one another, and so much the more, as ye see the day approaching."* As I shared verses, I have heard amazing stories of how God orchestrated the timing of truth sent and how others passed verses on as it mushroomed into this amazing ministry even from my bed of illness.

Another principle was listening to good music and dwelling on the words. Phrases like *"Not to the strong is the battle! Not to the Swift is the race, but to the true and the faithful victory is promised through grace"* (Fanny Crosby). And *"God is too wise to be mistaken! God is too good to be unkind! So when you don't understand, when you can't see His plan, when you can't trace His hand, trust His heart"* (Babbie Mason) became life sustaining to me. Dwelling on truth, beauty, goodness and righteousness, like Philippians 4:8 says, really does make a difference! I, at times, wearied of my debilitating weakness. One particularly frustrating day, I was grouching about things to My Loving Savior, feeling like I could agree with Job: *"For destruction from God was a terror to me, and by reason of His highness I could not endure"* (Job 21:23). I glanced sideways at a verse flipchart I had and read: *"Listen to me, you whom I have upheld since you were conceived and have carried since your birth, even to old age I am HE; and to gray hairs, I will bear you. I have made and I will sustain you; even I will carry, and will deliver you"* (Isaiah 46:3-4). I did not want to live till my hair was grey! I was ready to simply fall asleep and wake up in heaven because I was so worn out pushing through the dizziness, fatigue and weakness each day. I was trying to do it on my own. Verses like 2 Timothy 2:3 *"Thou therefore endure hardness, as a good soldier of Jesus Christ"* were discouraging rather than enabling because I was weary in the process.

Then one middle-mile day, I was watching a dog-training video. The trainer, who was working with an especially troubled anxious little dog, had taken him into the open courtyard with dogs of all sizes. When the dog would not be still, the trainer gently forced him to lay down at his feet in what seemed to be an absolutely defenseless position. Any attempt to stand and defend himself was stopped by the trainer. When another dog would attempt to bother him, the trainer would prevent it. That dog lay there quivering for a time and then slowly began to relax as it sensed that no harm would come to him as long as he lay there under the care of the trainer. Soon other dogs were coming to sniff him and he did not stir. He knew the master had control of the entire situation and he trusted him completely. The picture of how God works with us was evident to me in a way I had not seen before my long illness. In Matthew 27:14, Jesus was perfectly silent in His hour of greatest trial. God allows trials to help us to learn to stop being anxious and simply be still before our only Source of help—Him. God invites us to, *"Come unto me all you who labor and are heavy-laden and I will give you rest"* (Matthew 11:28) and to *"Call unto me, and I will answer thee, and shew thee great and mighty things, which thou knowest not"* (Jeremiah 33:3). We can call when we are in trouble and learn His mighty truths. We endure trials because they help us to learn more of Him (Psalm 112:7). We are exhorted to not grow weary while doing good for in due season we will reap if we don't faint (Galatians 6:9; 2 Thessalonians 3:13). Paul told us to run with endurance the race set before us, fixing our eyes on Jesus the Author and Finisher of our faith (Hebrews 12:1-2).

God's story of my life is not finished. I still must take one day at a time, fixing my eyes on Jesus, my strength, relying on the promise *"Faithful is He (Jesus) who promised, who also will do it"* (1 Thessalonians 5:24). My body has finally readjusted to the effects of the drug interactions and, after five years waking every morning to incredible fatigue and dizziness, I have days when I wake feeling better. Each day I still claim the verse, *"I can do all things through Christ who strengthens me"* (Philippians 4:13). It really is true that when we have no strength, God is the strength in our weakness. I recently read the story of Gideon in Judges 8:4 when he was *"weary yet pursuing"* the enemies of Israel. Despite those who mocked and refused to support him when he asked for help, he was victorious. We keep pressing on for the sake of Jesus Christ. We endure for the prize of being called *"faithful"* when we stand before the Lord. *"Behold, we count them happy which endure"* (2 Thessalonians 1:4). *"Ye have heard of the patience of Job, and have seen the end of the Lord; that the Lord is very pitiful, and of tender mercy"* (James 5:11). When will the final healing take place? I don't know. I simply remember what Amy Carmichael once said, *"Cannot God be silent with His most trusted servants?"* ENDURANCE *is trusting when you don't have answers.*

It's the middle mile again.

STRATEGIES FOR BUILDING YOUR ENDURANCE

1. List your key *"take away(s)"* that you learned from this chapter?

_____

_____

_____

_____

2. Based on what you learned, what small change can you make today to help you develop ENDURANCE?

Emotionally

Spiritually

Physically

_____

_____

_____

_____

3. Are you intentionally sharing at least one verse that God has used to grow you, daily, or at least weekly, with the important people in your life? Will you consider developing this habit to watch God grow it?

_____

_____

_____

_____

4. Do you feel *"weary and wanting to quit,"* or are you like Gideon, *"weary and still pursuing"* by God's grace? If you feel like quitting, take some time to dwell on 2 Corinthians 12:9-10. Thank God that He is your sufficiency when you have none on your own.

_____

_____

_____

_____

5. Is there a person in your world who comes to mind that you could encourage this week? Will you make the point to write that note, make that call, send that text or go see them this week?

_____

_____

_____

_____

6. What are you doing now that helps you endure, and what changes can you make to help you stay strong in the *"Middle Mile?"*

_____

_____

_____

_____

ABOUT RUTH E. MEED

 Ruth E. Meed was born the first of twin girls in Ethiopia, and at age 9 moved with her family to Ontario, Canada and then on to New Brunswick, where she finished her school years. She earned a Diploma of Biblical and Theological Studies from New Brunswick Bible Institute, a BA in Counseling from Washington Bible College, an MAT in Special Education and MEd in Biblical Counseling from Bob Jones University. Ruth is a *"Highly Qualified"* certified Special Educator. She also has John Maxwell Leadership Certification.

Local Church ministry has been her life mission, including opportunities for the service to her Lord as an AWANA youth club leader/Director, and singing in choirs and other music groups. Her experiences include: acting as the resident social worker in a group home for girls in Manchester, NH, teaching in Greenville County, SC and Bob Jones Academy in Special Education Classrooms, 3rd-8th grade and most recently as an Assistant Professor of Education in the Special Ed Division at Bob Jones University, for a total of 25 years teaching and making a difference in the lives of young people.

During the last seven years, significant health challenges have given her a toolbox of perspectives on the meaning of endurance. She still travels speaking and consulting at various venues in North America on a restricted basis and has also traveled to Africa to teach as God gives strength.

Contact Ruth:
- Website: www.Meeditations.blog
- LinkedIn: www.LinkedIn.com/in/Ruth-Meed-8942ab1b
- Email: Ruth.Meed@gmail.com

THE RACE ISN'T OVER UNTIL YOU WIN

By Edward Reed

THE RACE ISN'T OVER UNTIL YOU WIN

Endurance – The ability to withstand hardship, setbacks, and obstacles to achieve your desired outcome.

The race isn't over until you win.

Do you ever feel like life has tossed you into a race that you weren't prepared to run? Do you have desired outcomes for yourself, family or team? You are not alone, people all over the world feel like they are running in this race we call *Life*. We all have things we want to accomplish but sometimes there are hardships, setbacks and obstacles that attempt to become barriers in our lives. In this chapter, we are going to share a few stories, develop a winning strategy and clarify important goals you have for yourself.

Before we go forward, let's identify the competition. Take out a mirror. Look directly into the eyes of the person staring back at you in the mirror. Next, go above the eyes, right into the forehead. You should have seen your brain. This is where your competitors live. Your top competitors are your beliefs, perceptions, attitude and thinking. Our outcomes are determined by our decisions.

In 2001, one of my students had great odds working against him to graduate his senior year. Life was not fair. His father was out of the picture by choice and his mother was desperate to see her son graduate from high school. My student wrestled with his perceptions of his ability and the destructive decisions he made throughout high school which lead him to a situation requiring a major turnaround. Prior to starting his senior year, I met with his assistant principal and mother to discuss my student's situation. He needed to take 7 classes during the day and 4 classes at night. His mother started to cry, as the reality of the weight of his challenge became clear. Her true fear was her son dropping out of school and quickly going on a downward spiral. The assistant principal was doubtful. I was highly motivated by believing in the words of Napoleon Hill, *"Whatever your mind can conceive believe the mind can achieve regardless of how many times you may have failed in the past."*

My student needed a victorious strategy beyond just a list of classes he needed to pass. We had to tap into his mindset. Our team had to equip him to defeat his inner competitors, so he could execute the winning game plan. Imagine this was you or your child. Think about what is at stake. If you were mom, what would do and what messages would you send to yourself? Imagine being the student, struggling with self-esteem, hurt and anger because your dad left your mom and has had nothing to do with you since your early childhood. The reality was clear. He could drown in sorrow or tune in to a different channel. I wrote out the plan 11 classes, 7 during the day and 4 at night (2 on Mondays and Wednesday; 2 on Tuesdays and Thursdays). My job was to build a strong team committed to winning. The team had to believe our student was going to beat the odds. The deciding factor to *endure* this storm was making the decision to move forward and work through the process.

In the beginning, deep down my student wanted to graduate despite all the messages in his mind telling him that he was incapable of passing so many classes. On a personal note, I knew if I could leverage my relationship with him to get inside of his heart and mind, we could withstand the hardships and change the message. My strategy was to work with him weekly, letting success become his primary motivator. For the next 10 months, I encouraged him and held him accountable to position himself to reach his desired outcome despite the challenge. Throughout the process, there was anxiety of failure that turned into expectation of succeeding. The tears of hurt and frustration turned into tears of joy and celebration. I exposed my student to a different way of thinking. He made the decision to tune into the *"I'm possible"* station and removed *"impossible"* from his playlist. I am honored to say that my student graduated with his class on time. By the way, the assistant principal bet me a steak dinner that my student wouldn't graduate. As a champion for the next generation, I accepted the bet knowing losing was not an option. After winning, I declined the steak dinner while enjoying the taste of victory. You see, I had more at stake than a juicy steak. I didn't leave my corporate career to become a school counselor with losing as an option.

Perhaps you or someone you care about needs a winning strategy to overcome obstacles hindering desired outcomes.

The first step in reaching your desired outcome is to visualize the victory. Look beyond the obstacles that are immediately in front of you until you see a favorable outcome. We are talking about strengthening your faith. See the victory before you go into battle. As one attempts to be positive, understand your inner adversary will send you messages in an attempt to keep you from moving forward. There will be messages saying, *"You know you aren't good enough."* *"What makes you think you are so special?"* *"Look at your record, you can't do anything worthwhile."* But wait. There is a champion inside of you too. The champion inside of you wants to tell you, *"You were made with a purpose, designed to succeed."* *"There is more to life than remaining in your status-quo."* *"Look at all the things you've learned from past failure. Turn the past into your stepping stones."* Making the choice to believe in what you can't see in the moment, yet knowing in your spirit it is possible, will allow you to move forward. Repeat this statement, *"My victory starts with my vision!"*

Second, we have to continuously focus on each stroke of our paintbrush as we are painting the picture of our vision coming to life. In today's world, there are several things competing for your attention and time. Take a moment and write out a list of the things that are competing for your attention. Next, rank your list in terms of where to spend the most time to the least amount of time. While reviewing your rankings, how is time invested on your top six moving you toward reaching your desired outcomes? In the group of six, what should be replaced? It's time to refocus. Make a new list of where you need to invest your allocation of time. (Understand you are making an investment versus spending. When we invest, we expect a return. When we spend, we are not looking for a return—it is simply an act of consumption.) Rank your list 1-6. This is your focus point. For the next 30 days, *focus your attention on your priorities.*

Third, see the picture and focus in on your target: it is time to *gain wisdom.* Ask yourself, *"Who do I know or need to know who has accomplished what it is I want to accomplish?"* Let's go! These people exist or maybe you are getting ready to be the first one. Remember, most of the things we enjoy today were created by someone who had a vision to create what didn't already exist. Take out a piece of paper, make three columns. Label Column One *"My Network."* Write down the names of people in your network who are doing what you want to do. Label Column Two *"My Extended Network."* Write down the names of people who are not in your network, but are a part of your network's network and are doing what you want to do. Label Column Three *"Experts in the Field."* Write down the names of people who have done what you want to do but are not connected to your network. With these three lists, your task is to learn from each one of these people. Some of them might share a simple nugget of wisdom. Others might become part of your circle of influence and sources of motivation. Make sure you do something in return to add value to those who add value to you. For the experts in the field, learn from their books, videos, podcasts and workshops. Remember you are investing in wisdom seeds. These seeds are more valuable than plant seeds. Produce from the plant feeds the body. Fruit from wisdom feeds the mind. Don't allow yourself to suffer from mental malnutrition.

Fourth, one of the most important components of a winning strategy is my favorite verb, *"Action."* It is foolish to see the image, focus on priorities, have access to wisdom and fail to *take action.* Get excited. You are a person of action. The fact that you are reading this book demonstrates that you take action in pursuit of achieving your goals. For me, cranking up the engine and putting the truck in drive was my challenge. I am highly motivated—knowing what I want and where I want to go. Networking has become easy for me. My problem was finding the right fuel to put in the tank. Well, I found it and I am still looking for the upgrade. This fuel is called, *"Get off your butt and start moving."* Warning, warning! You can get paralysis from over-analysis. Over the years and even today, I have to accept the reality that success is acquired by the actions we take. How often do you have good intentions buried in the graveyard of your mind? Where would you be right now if you acted on those good intentions? How would your situation be different? Whose life would have been positively impacted?

Over the years, I've been fortunate to learn leadership and personal development from Dr. John C. Maxwell. John is recognized as one of the top leadership and personal development experts in the world. One of the best lessons I've learned and continue to teach in my masterclasses comes from John's book, *"Intentional Living: Choosing a Life that Matters."* In his book, John discusses why good intentions aren't enough. Good intentions are desires. Without action, they will never become results. You are on your way to achieving your desired outcome as you master the art of endurance. As a former runner, the only way I crossed the finish line was moving forward. Forward movement is the result of taking action.

A few tips begin with:

1. Identify what specific tasks are required to move you forward.

2. Using your calendar, schedule time for the action by putting it on your calendar with all the other important appointments.

3. Inspect, protect and respect your schedule. As this becomes a habit, you will experience an increase in your productivity.

4. If this is already a habit for you, what do you need to do to strengthen the quality of time spent on this activity?

5. Looking back at your calendar for the past 30 days, make a list of the top ten things you intended to do but didn't get around to scheduling and implementing the ideas. Where could you have scheduled the necessary actions to move forward with your ideas? No worries.

6. Look at the month ahead, schedule your actions steps now. Our goal is continuous growth and improvement.

Recently, I've been blessed to receive awards and recognition for the work I've been doing in the area of personal development to help others and teams improve their lives. One of my biggest challenges has been finding time to do all the things I want to do. My passion runs deep, my network is growing, my work continues to produce positive results and I consistently invest in my personal development.

My goal is to be one of the best in my field to maximize my ability to help others. Sounds good right? Here is the other side. I am a husband, dad and strong man of faith. I spent many years and hours working as a leader in my church and in my local school system at the expense of my family.

Naturally, I encountered new barriers that I didn't anticipate. My definition of manhood was to serve God in the church and to provide for your family. Overtime, I am learning that manhood is not defined by simply working in the church and providing for your family. Manhood is about being the person God created you to be.

Every person is a gift from God, born with gifts that have to be developed. These gifts have the ability to improve our global community, if we use them for good and not evil. Being blessed with the responsibility of being a spouse and parent gives us a chance to learn and grow daily. There are several times when I have fallen short. Sometimes, I try to jump over the hurdle only to trip and fall flat on my face. It is in those moments, I made time to reflect, think, learn and get back in the game.

An important component of a winning game plan is prioritizing your values. My top four priorities are God, myself, family and service. Why this order? Without God, I am nothing. Next in line, I must invest in being my best self so I can be the best husband, dad and service provider. I choose family before service because, if I neglect my family in the pursuit of my passion and purpose, I minimize my effectiveness to serve others. Finally, service is a priority because through service I honor God, personally grow, contribute to building healthy communities and generate resources to bless my family and others.

In the first half of 2017, I was very intentional and hungry to learn about making major life transitions from two of the people I admire the most – John Maxwell and Les Brown. Les Brown is one of the top motivational speakers in the world.

In my conversation with John, I asked him, *"When you were making the transition from being a pastor to doing what you are doing now, what were some of the biggest obstacles you encountered and what did you do to overcome those obstacles as you pursued your passion and purpose?"*

John replied, *"Well, first of all Ed, it was the hardest transition I ever had to make. You see it took me about three years. When you hear me teach the 5 Levels of Leadership—to be honest with you when I left the pastorate, I was on level 5 with pastors. When I left that and went over into the secular business community, I went back to level 1. That was very hard on me because I wanted to tell the people who didn't know and didn't care how wonderful I was, they didn't know and didn't care and that is when I realized, it doesn't matter what you did yesterday. When you make a transition, you better be ready to do it again today. I went back to the basics. I had to prove myself again. I had no credit that I'm carrying over. I had no right to be respected. I had to earn my respect. Respect is earned on different ground. So I did my homework, asked a lot of questions, and I took a lot of notes. I learned, I studied, I observed, I watched, I tried. I failed, I retried again after I learned, and it took me about three years. Maybe the hardest part was, to be honest with you, not only did nobody really care that I had to start back at level 1, but all of a sudden I lost my identity. I lost all the things I was in the Christian community. I wasn't in the Christian community anymore. I left the people who loved me and put me on level 5. I went to a group of people who put me on level 1 and said, 'I'm not sure you can get to level 2, but you can give it a shot if you want to.' That was one of the greatest transitions for me. It caused me to learn that this was very difficult and very humbling. As I look back at that time, what it did for me was, it said, 'If I lost it all tomorrow, give me about a month and I will figure out how to come back again.' Because I think everybody needs to lose something to know they can gain it back. I just think there is something healthy about that. It gave me a lot of confidence in myself. It gave me a lot of self-respect. As I got it back, what was great was it came quicker. Once I got in there, it took about 3 years, I was able to climb the 5 levels a lot quicker. I am still not a 5 [being humble, John is one of the very best]. I already knew what to anticipate and I knew what I had done the first time. I just had to connect it over to a different context. It was very challenging and I'm absolutely glad I did it. If I had not done it, there wouldn't be a John Maxwell Team."*

A few months later, along with a small group of leaders, we spent time with Les Brown in Houston, Texas. I shared my background and passion with Les, asking him to share his wisdom on how I could leap into living out my next dream. Les replied, *"Make the commitment."* He then shared a story with me that motivated him to launch forward. He was in the audience listening to someone on stage say, *"There is someone here that is supposed to be doing what I'm up here doing, but you have discouraged yourself, and you know who you are. There is someone here and this is your passion. You see, I love making money, I've made over ten million dollars doing this but you, you love this. This gives your life meaning, value and purpose and you know who you are. Now, I'm just going to say this and I'm not going to say anything more. The only reason I'm up here holding this microphone and your seated out there is I represent the thoughts you have rejected for yourself."* Les went on to encourage me to make the leap, sharing the message he told his mentor, *"I am not going to reject myself anymore!"*

So what have I learned? Life is not going to be fair, no matter how good or bad others might think we are. We have daily challenges. No one really knows the depths of the demons we wrestle, unless we share our story. The good news is, as long as you and I are among the breathing, we have the ability to endure whatever life throws at us. Through faith, we create the vision, taking action so we can win. The race isn't over until you cross the finish the line. I love you and pray for your success as you press forward. God bless!

STRATEGIES FOR BUILDING YOUR ENDURANCE

1. Vision – As you visualize your victory, think about the image you see. What is taking place? Who is involved? What are the results? Take a moment and write out a personalized vision statement for the race you are about to win.

_____

_____

_____

_____

2. Priorities – Based on your vision, what are your priorities to accomplishing this challenging yet doable task? What three habits will you change to stay focused on achieving your desired outcome?

_____

_____

_____

_____

3. Network – Who is on your team? What role will they play? What role needs to be filled? What will you do today to fill the role with the right person?

_____

_____

_____

_____

4. Action Plan – Knowledge, insight and wisdom are tools at your disposable to help you endure. Now it is time for you to take action. Does your action plan clearly identify action steps with timelines for you to complete as you move along your course?

_____

_____

_____

_____

ABOUT EDWARD REED

Ed Reed is a humble leader, who overcame challenges, setbacks and other barriers. Ed credits his success to his faith, parents, professors, mentors and coaches for equipping him with the skills and mindset necessary for beating the odds of attaining success.

Ed is the Founder and CEO of Academic Management Group, LLC – a small business providing coaching, strategic educational and career planning, consulting, personality and career interest assessments and leadership development training services. He currently serves on various advisory boards for nonprofit organizations including the 2016 - 2017 President of the Maryland School Counselor Association. Ed also serves his community by leading the School Counseling department for his local middle school. He has served in various leadership roles in private industry and in secondary schools that have been recognized as among the top 100 schools in America and top 6 secondary schools in Maryland.

Ed is a certified John C. Maxwell International Executive Coach, Leadership Trainer and Keynote Speaker. He is living a life of significance by adding value to others.

Contact Edward:
- Website: www.AcademicManagementGroup.com
- Website: www.JohnMaxwellgroup.com/EdwardReed
- Facebook: www.Facebook.com/AcademicManagementGroupLLC
- Twitter: www.Twitter.com/EReedSpeaks
- Email: EReed@AcademicManagementGroup.com
- Phone: 301-335-6689

THE WONDERFUL RACE
By Carlos Vargas

THE WONDERFUL RACE

"I have fought the good fight, I have finished the race,
I have kept the faith."
2 Timothy 4:7

"There is no secret to success. It is the result of preparation, hard work and learning from failure, loyalty and persistence." Colin Powell, 65th United States Secretary Of State

There is a very interesting television show called *"The Amazing Race"* in which teams of two people race around the world in competition with other teams. Contestants strive to arrive first at *"Pit Stops"* at the end of each leg of the race to win prizes and to avoid coming in last (which carries the possibility of elimination or a significant disadvantage in the following leg). Contestants travel to and within multiple countries in a variety of transportation modes, including airplanes, hot air balloons, helicopters, trucks, bicycles, taxicabs, cars, trains, buses, boats and on foot. Clues provided in each leg lead the teams to the next destination or direct them to perform a task, either together or by a single member. These challenges are related in some manner to the country wherein they are located or its culture. Teams are progressively eliminated until three are left; at that point, the team that arrives first in the final leg is awarded the grand prize.

One of the most interesting things about this show is how many people think that it is easy to complete the race. Some of the contestants are couples or friends, but most of them have *underestimated* the amount of *endurance* needed to complete the job ahead of them.

It is amazing how much we *underestimate the effort* needed to lead ourselves, teams and families, and *overestimate* the *result of our intentions*.

Paul, when he wrote to Timothy, used the analogy of a race. He used the expression *"I have finished the race."* In order to finish the race, he has to first of all *"place"* to race it before he can finish it. As leaders, it is critical to know where we are going before we start.

The 5K Race – should I get on the bus or not?

When I was younger, I had the opportunity to sign up for a 5K race in my beautiful island of Puerto Rico. I was young and had no idea what the word *"training"* meant. My physical education teacher told me to train every day. He kept reminding the class of the date for the race. I had three months to prepare but, as normal kid, I did not listen to my teacher. Time passed by and training was replaced with video games, riding my bike and doing things that I considered pleasant. From my perspective, training for the race was not important or anything I looked forward to. When the day for the race arrived, I was so excited for the race. I was certain that there was no way for me to be the fastest. My expectations were that I would not be the last one either.

As the race began, I started competing to stay with the group and gave it all I had. I pressed on, passing some of my friends from school. It felt good to be with the group and not in the back. Shortly thereafter, my body started reacting a little bit weird. All of a sudden, I could feel my energy tank was getting low. My muscles screamed *"What are you doing?"* I started to fall back in the group to the degree that I started to walk with a group of guys and girl that were in the back.

What happened? I was so certain that I would be OK for the race. My intentions to finish the race were there and I desired it.

But, there was something I had missed. Just like Solomon says in Proverbs 29:18, *"without vision, the people perish."* To tell you the truth, I had no vision of the race. All that I was focusing on was having fun with my friends. I had not planned or visualized what was needed to complete the race. After a couple of minutes, a bus passed by us to pick up anyone that was exhausted and that could not continue the race. Most of the people got on the bus. There was something inside me that was pushing me to keep on going. Even though I would be the last one, I needed to keep on going. Even though I was in the last group to cross the finish line, that experience taught me a lot.

There are three key things to learn from this experience that I would like to share:

1.We need to identify the starting line and what is needed to get there.

As leaders, we will be in the race of life. Many times, we are invited to be part of the race and we say yes without thinking. It is ok to be available and willing to lead. It is absolutely necessary to identify what is needed for you to get to the starting line. Is there something you need to prepare ahead of time? Do you need to train your body, mind or spirit, in order to be ready to withstand the pressures of the race? Athletes wake up early in the morning and go through strict exercise and dietary restrictions in order to prepare their body for their sport or race. What do you need to do be ready before you get to the starting line?

2. We need to prepare ahead of time if we want to be in the race.

Preparation is the key. The 65th United States Secretary of State, Colin Powell said: *"There is no secret to success. It is the result of preparation, hard work and learning from failure, loyalty and persistence.*" To endure whatever comes our way, we need to be prepared ahead of time. Our teams will look to us as models. If we are prepared, they will prepare themselves. If we are not prepared, they will not do anything, but follow our example. What are you doing to be ready? What are you doing to prepare yourself to endure the challenges that come your way? Bill Hybels says in his book *Simplify*: "*You need to fill in your buckets ahead of time and keep them full. If not, nobody else will come and fill them up for you.*"

3. We need to be ready for the unexpected.

As in my race, we have the opportunity to take shortcuts—to get on the bus to finish the race. But we need to be ready to do whatever it takes to finish. The unexpected in us can manifest in different ways. Every leader needs to be aware that unexpected situations will appear. The question is: How will we respond to them? Those unexpected situations are the ones that define us and reveal our character to those around us.

What is my desire to achieve my goal?

In a race, you start with a vision, you see yourself crossing the finish line and in proportion to that is how you start to develop your plan. How much effort you put into reaching your vision is the desire that you have to reach out your goal.

Napoleon Hill, famous author of the book, *Think and Grow Rich*, says: "*You must have a burning desire in order to go and reach your goal*" Why a *burning* desire? We know that every time we are in motion, we are facing opposition. The earth gravity is pulling us down and slowing us down. Other people may be against us because of our views or ideas. Lack of funding or budgets can be a hindrance, too.

In the spiritual realm, the Bible says in Ephesians 6:12 that our fight is against rulers and principalities. Daniel had to wait for his answer because it had been detained by one of those spiritual rulers.

It is not until we have a burning desire to endure whatever comes that we will be able to lead in the middle of difficulties. I remember many years ago, while working for a Fortune 100 company, I lead a project that saved the company millions of dollars. I am not talking about a small amount. We are talking in the range of over 100 million dollars in a five year period. Even though I was recognized and everyone came to our division to see how we were achieving and exceeding all the goals, my team was questioned for not following the company standard.

You probably have faced this before. My burning desire was not to follow a set of rules, but to reach the best utilization of our datacenter and enable our customers to get the best return on investment possible. After I was recognized for the amazing achievements, I was invited to a couple of meetings to explain what my team did and how we achieved all the savings. At one point in time, I counted 75 meetings to explain why we did not follow the company standard.

My friend, if my desire or my why was not clear, I could have forgotten my reason for doing what I was doing. My desire was what kept me going and then something amazing happened. My desire then became contagious. In less than one year, the company that I worked for saw the value of my vision and promoted me to be the head architect across all of its divisions. Without knowing what you need to do, it will be almost impossible for you to endure your leadership role and to significantly make an impact for your team, family or church.

There are three things that I learned from that experience:

1. Your desire when communicated can fuel the transformation that is needed.

As a leader, you are recognized for your contributions, and when you start impacting others, you move up the ladder of your influence. Many times, people are waiting for someone that will bring the challenge that will champion and move them forward. Your desire, when it is burning inside of you, will move you and will also help you to move others. All that is needed to start a movement is someone to start it. Your burning desire is the one that will do that. Jesus has been the greatest leader in the history of our planet. In the book of Acts 5:36-38, Gamaliel says: *"...leave these men alone—if this is from God, it will prosper."* The disciples had a burning desire to communicate what Jesus did and they were the fuel needed to start the transformation. Over two thousand years later, we are still reaping the effect of the burning desire instilled in them and by them.

2. Your desire will be challenged by others that want to stay in their comfort zone.

It is easy to stay in the same spot doing the same thing over and over and over. Albert Einstein, one of the greatest minds of the 20th century, offers this perspective: *"Insanity is doing the same thing over and over again, but expecting different results."* Haven't you met people like this? As a leader, when you are bringing change, you will be challenged by a sinking feeling. In doing the same thing over and over again, people will say—*"Why do we need to change?"*

As a leader that goes the distance, it is your duty to wake up those under your leadership by not accepting the lethargic sleep that keeps them in their comfort zone. As leader, you will endure harsh conditions but, at the end of the day, your reward is to see all those that were sleeping and stuck in their comfort zone are now awake and rejoicing because you brought them back to life.

3. Your desire is yours, never forget that.

Others may try to challenge you or even try to make you change your desire, so they don't look bad. But you must always remember that what is driving you has to be consuming you literally like fire all over you. Then and only then will you be able to push everything else aside. Never forget that other people will not see your vision in the same way you do and that is OK.

As an enduring trailblazing leader, you are different than everyone else, you are investing in your dreams, you are investing in your team, and you are reaping the benefit of it. So remember, you set the pace for your dream. Only you can keep it alive or allow it to be extinguished.

Do you know the path that you will take in your race?

In order to finish the race, you need to know where it is that you are going to go. You need to chart the course that you will navigate. International Author, Speaker, Coach and Pastor, John C. Maxwell has called this *"The Law of Navigation."* You need to know the way to chart the course so others can then follow you. To participate in a race, you need to know the equipment that is needed. If you are in a marathon, you will need certain gear (shirt, shorts, racing shoes). But if you are in a mushing race in Alaska, you will need a sled, racing dogs, snow boots, snow gear and much more. As you can see, both races have something in common: a starting line and a finishing line. You need to start and finish, but that is where the similarities end.

As a leader, you need to be able to chart the course and plan ahead for everything that will come your way. Mentor, speaker and self-made multi-millionaire, Paul Martinelli says: *"The best plans have one step."* Sometimes, in the planning phase, we try to plan so much that we never start. But, if we can learn to have short simple plans and put them into action, we can learn to develop a continual winning pattern.

When God spoke to Joshua, He gave them a simple and effective plan to take over Jericho. Phase One started with walking—one single step followed by another one, then continue walking completely around the city—once each day for six days. It was a simple plan that was completely dependent on God. As leaders, we need to remember that we will formulate the plan and we need to be in constant connection with our Father in heaven, so we can submit all our plans to Him. He needs to be leading us and leading our plans.

Joshua and the people completed Phase One on the sixth day. Day seven started the same way as the previous six days—together, they all walked in silence around Jericho, so they executed the plan—simply and perfectly. God instructed Joshua that, on day seven when the priests blew their horns, everyone was to shout. They had the plan and Joshua as their leader executed the plan. We can learn that without the plan, we will not be able to lead our team, family or church. We will not be able to endure what we will face. But, when we follow and complete the plan, we will receive the blessing of it like what Joshua experienced. In Joshua 6:20, we see the results to following the plan. The walls of the city of Jericho fell down. Joshua experienced what he expected. We need to remember that if we want to succeed we need to develop our plan and follow the plan—but first of all, we must submit our plans to God. He has the last word. He can change, alter or modify our plans, but we need to do our part and He will do his.

Just as with the Israelites, some people may question your plan.

We need to be ready for that. Remember, we are all humans and all the good things we have experienced are forgotten very quickly. The Lord made the Israelites cross the Red Sea to save them from slavery. Everyone that came behind them was swallowed by waves when the Red Sea closed. But soon they forgot those miracles and desired to be back in slavery because it was secure; it was their comfort zone. Your people may react in the same way, so make your plan, act on your plan and follow your plan. You will see the reward on the other side of the finish line.

Consistency wins all the time.

As a kid, I grew up watching wrestling matches. As an adult, one my favorite wrestlers was The Rock (Dwayne Johnson). His slogan was *"The Rock has come back to"* and he would mention the city's name. It is interesting because he was very consistent. He kept that slogan everywhere that he went.

Once The Rock was asked to what he attributed his success and he answered: *"Success isn't always about greatness. It's about consistency. Consistent hard work leads to success. Greatness will come."* And that is so true.

To win in a race, the athletes have to wake up early and do their exercise to get their body in shape. Then, they need to eat correctly and cut out some things. Then, after that, they need to practice their sport. You need to practice your sport. In the same way, you need to develop your talent or craft. A consistent leader will be recognized because he will continue making headway even though others don't. When we are consistent, it means that our success and plans will continue getting better. But you will also encounter some failure on the way. That is OK. Your failures will be the fuel that will help you achieve greater success with your team.

A couple of months ago, I decided that it was time for a change. I hit my twentieth birthday for the second time and I was not in the best shape of my life. So I started to develop a plan to get in shape. At the beginning, it was challenging, but I had already decided to be consistent. Instead of focusing on the short term gain, I chose to focus on the long term vision of having perfect health. Across the months, I did not see the physical change my consistency was creating, but other people did. I saw a change in my work, emotions, eating habits and mood. And I went to the doctor and for my surprise I found out that I had lost thirty pounds. After all the exams and tests, everything was in great shape. All the levels were in the green. My vision was not to be in the green, but it was to have perfect health. I have kept making progress since then. I learned to be consistent and enjoy life. Then, I had a result that was recognized by others.

As leaders, we need to be consistent with our teams. It is not the size of the steps that matters. What matters is that we are consistently taking steps forward to reach our goal and work on our plans.

ACT

When we hear the word *"act"*, we normally think in terms of doing and moving. I want to use the word as an acronym:

A for Accomplishments. As leaders, we accomplish a lot of things. Big and small, but most of the time, we do not take the time to recognize those accomplishments. Our teams need to hear from us when they have done something good. In order to help each other to win the race, it is needed for them to hear what they are doing correctly.

C is for Celebrate. When the team has completed a task or a milestone, celebrate it. It does not have to be something big, but celebrating by leaving out early, having extra time for themselves, or whatever idea you can use, so your team can celebrate is critical for the morale of the team. This also applies to families and churches.

In one of the volunteer organizations that I participate in, we have a techy night where we come together once a month to celebrate all the great things that we have accomplished in that month. It is just a couple of guys and girls having a good time, but recognizing what brought us together that night. So try something new and different to celebrate what you are recognizing.

Last but not least, *T is for Transformation*. What needs to be transformed, modified or changed? What is not delivering the expected outcome? Sometimes, we focus on this one thing more than any other, but we need to have all three in order to help our team succeed. To transform, your team needs to first feel that what they are doing is good (accomplishments), then celebrate them and lastly improve to transform.

Athletes in a race look at their accomplishments as they complete their training every day and they celebrate when they accomplish a better time in their race. If something is not working, they transform it. When I started to exercise, I was able to walk 1 mile an hour. I was out of breath by the end, but it was an accomplishment and I celebrated it. After a while, I kept on going and started getting better from one and a half mile to two miles. Then something happened. My calves started to complain. I needed to transform. So I got better shoes to walk with and I went from two miles, to three miles and now I can do four miles per hour. But, it was only after looking at the small accomplishments, celebrating them, and then transforming my body to reach the goal of perfect health. Remember that what you do is what others will do. Your team will mirror what you model for them, so you start the chain reaction for them.

Why is this happening to me?

After you experience some success, you may feel that you are in a cloud. You say I paid the price, I deserve this. And, you are mostly right. This is a constant consistent journey of learning and adjusting.

I have a friend who is a commercial airline pilot. One day, we were talking about all the things he has to do to keep the plane stable and on track to get to the correct destination. He explained to me that he has to consistently adjust the different components, in order to compensate for all the external forces, just so he can take the plane safely from one airport to another.

As leaders, you will have to adjust, make adjustments constantly because of situations that happen to you or because of you. And at the end, they will help you get to your goal. Be sure to understand that there will be moments that you will have to adjust and you may get disappointed. But don't worry! Jesus already said these words to us in John 16:33: *"In this world, you will have trouble, but I have overcome the world."* So, when you get discouraged or things get tough, get up and keep on going. Superstar Coach Vince Lombardi once said: *"It's not whether you get knocked down; it's whether you get up"* that counts.

Who is in your bus?

When we are preparing to race, we need to have the correct people on our team. We need people that will support us, not slow us down. When you look at your leadership, everyone is valuable, but not everyone should be in your bus. Your bus should have the people that, if needed, will get out of the bus and push the bus so it can get to its destination. In your bus, you want to have the people that will help you finish the race, not the ones that will complain because things are done in a different way or because they get scared.

This reminds me of the story of the twelve spies. In the Bible book of Numbers, chapter 13, we have a wonderful story to illustrate this point. Twelve spies were sent to look at the land of Canaan. This land was promised to the people of Israel. God was sending them in because it was time to collect on it. But when ten of the twelve spies came back, they brought a bad report. Ten spies who did not get the vision from God, even though they were seeing the signs of the promise. In verse 27, the spies said: *"..the land flows with milk and honey."* They saw it with their own eyes, but did not believe the promise God gave them. They focused on the circumstances that were around them.

In our race, we will have people that will be like the spies; they will focus on circumstances, problems and situations. As a leader, you want to spot those people and get them off of your bus. Because, if you don't get them off your bus, you probably will have a similar outcome to what happened to the people of Israel. Because of the influence of the ten spies, the people of Israel that believed them did not see the Promised Land. Your strategy in the race is to bring alongside you the ones who will help you, the ones who are catching the vision that God has given you. You want next to you the people who have the spirit of Joshua and Caleb, the ones who will get up and will believe in the vision, the ones who (even though they have to grow) will continue to follow the vision and allow it to mold them. And at the correct time, when it is your time to move on, they can continue the vision and complete the race for you just as Joshua did for Moses.

Who is with me?

Who is with you is very important. To win a race, you need a team. That team is the one that will be together in good times and in the challenging times. There is an African proverb that says: *"If you want to go fast go alone, but if you want to go far, go together."* That is absolutely true.

In order to finish the race, there are five questions that I ask myself when I want to win a race. You should ask yourself these five questions that will help you identify the people that you need next to you in order to complete your race:

- Who do I need close to win the race?

- Who can help me train for the race?

- Who can run the race with me?

- Who is available and willing to support me throughout the race?

- Who do I need to let go, so I can run race?

These questions look simple, but their application into your leadership race is monumental. As international speaker Jim Rohn asserted: *"Everyone has value, but not everyone needs to be valuable to you."* As human beings, we are valuable, as people we have value, but we need to learn to identify the correct place for someone in our team. If there is no place in our team, our responsibility is to help them find the correct place for them and not feel bad for doing so.

Reaching the Finish Line

Now that we have understood what we have to do to train and run the race, now is time to do it. It's our race and we need to feel it. Your muscles will need to be exercised, you will sweat, you will get tired and you will want to quit. You need to feel what will happen when you cross the finish line. You will feel the projects, meeting deadlines, generating deliverables and many other components of your race as a leader. You need to feel them in order to run your race. Without them, it is not a race; you are just posing for a picture.

After you feel the pressure, you need to learn to enjoy it. The athlete trains very hard and they feel the effects of the race in their body. One of the most important details about the race is to enjoy it. If the athlete does not enjoy the race, he will not do it over and over. He will not get up early in the morning to train or travel across country to participate in different races. He does it because he enjoys it. We will encounter moments that our only option is to make a decision to enjoy the race. As leaders, it is our decision to enjoy the race. We will sweat, get tired, want to quit because of everything that happens but remember the words of Paul *"I have finished the race."* That means that he knew what you and I are going through. You are not alone; your team is there for you.

After you enjoy it, you need to share the experience with others. As an athlete, you will train with a partner or group of people. The reason for that is to make it fun and enjoyable. In the same way as leaders, sharing the experience with others makes our job and position more enjoyable, and helps us finish the race. Remember you are not alone in this journey. You have people close to you who are there to share your struggle and assist with your challenges. You also can have an external accountability partner or coach that will help you through this process.

After you finish the race you don't just stop running, now you reflect on what just happened. What you just did. Could you do it better? Could you have done something different? Remember that after you finish, it is just the beginning of a new race. So take a deep breath, reflect on what you did and how you can improve it and repeat the process. When many people complete a race or project, they decide to stop and not do anything else. Others decide to take a long break that stifles the momentum you gained in the race. As a leader, your success will be determined by your daily agenda. Yesterday ended last night. Do not *"just rest in the idea"* that you won one race. You need to look at your vision and plan, then start working on your next race. Apply all you learned from the previous race, so you can then repeat the words of Paul *"I have fought the good fight, I have finished the race, I have kept the faith."*

You can do it. I know you can. Don't try, just do it. You will win the race and will rejoice with all the amazing things God will do in your life!

STRATEGIES FOR BUILDING YOUR ENDURANCE

1. Have you considered that your life is a race and are you actively participating in it?

_____

_____

_____

_____

2. What are you doing to prepare yourself to run your race?

_____

_____

_____

_____

3. Life is full of experiences. List three in your race and why they are important to you in your race?

_____

_____

_____

_____

4. Your goal is to reach the finish line. What is your goal in life and what are you doing to achieve it?

_____

_____

_____

_____

5. In order to win the race, you need to know where you have to go and for how long. Do you know the path that you need to take in order to win your race and reach your goal?

_____

_____

_____

_____

6. Describe what you do on a day to day basis to be consistent in your walk with Christ and your race to reach your personal goal?

_____

_____

_____

7. List your last 3 accomplishments, how you celebrated them and what you learned to transform yourself?

_____

_____

_____

_____

ABOUT CARLOS VARGAS

 Living to Serve, Lead and to be a Technical Geek.

For the last 20 years, Carlos Vargas has impacted people's live through his speaking, teaching and inspiring individuals across Brazil, Mexico, Dominican Republic, Paraguay, Cuba, Puerto Rico, United States and Europe. Carlos loves being a Transformation agent for people who have current limiting beliefs in their business, personal and spiritual lives. This is the fuel which keep him going.

Carlos work with individual, family, groups and businesses to help them reduce stress and enjoy life, thru great interaction via their personality and individual leadership competencies.

Carlos Vargas earn his education in the Defenders of the Faith Theological Institute in Santurce Puerto Rico and later received over than 80 IT certifications during his successful career as an International Architect with different fortune 100 and 500 companies.

Carlos was part of a Elite team of world changers invited to traveled to Paraguay and transform the lives of 17,000 people by helping them transform their lives.

As International Leadership and Life Coach, he finished a Tour through the beautiful countries of Brazil and Cuba where he helps countless people to transform their limiting beliefs into new opportunities.

Contact Carlos:
- Website: www.CarlosVargas.com
- Website: www.VIPLeadershipGroup.com
- Facebook: www.Facebook.com/CarlosVargasVIP
- Facebook: www.Facebook.com/VIPLeadershipGroup
- Twitter: www.Twitter.com/cavarpe

YOU WANT ME TO DO WHAT?

WHAT?
THE FRUIT OF ENDURANCE IN CONFRONTATION

By Terry Wood

YOU WANT ME TO DO WHAT?
THE FRUIT OF ENDURANCE IN CONFRONTATION

"But the goal of our instruction is love from a pure heart
and a good conscience and a sincere faith."
1 Timothy 1:5

Think for a moment of the first thing that comes to mind when you hear the word *endurance*. For most people, the thought of a marathon runner, a tri-athlete, a competitive swimmer or perhaps an association with someone exerting physical energy over prolonged amount of time. In this chapter I would like to challenge consideration of the physical paradigm and compel you to think of how *endurance* can be applied in the mental, if not spiritual condition. For many of us, our *endurance* over a lifetime with relationships, with people and with lifestyles can be quite challenging and at times exhausting. Many of us cringe at the thought of physical endurance, as we are less than prone to the required discipline it takes to actually endure sustained effort over the long haul to finish well, much less the mental capacity to remain engaged through mental struggles and life's challenging circumstances.

What I would like to explore in moving forward is the concept of endurance as it relates to the *mental acumen of confrontation*. Many people ranging from the extreme introvert to the timid peacemaker perhaps struggle with the thought of confrontation. All too often, this struggle is real and needs to be addressed.

Are you a parent who grew up in a home where confrontation became the battleground for power and control? In my home growing up, it was means used to establish control and often times ended in a literal train wreck of damaged emotions and sometimes led to physical abuse. Emotions ran unfettered and high resulting in fractured relationships and over-the-top verbal episodes of torment and toxicity. Maybe you are the parent of an unruly child that needs to have boundaries established in order to foster an environment of personal growth and discipline. The very thought of establishing that environment causes some parents to flee in order to do anything except confront the child with plans for structure, responsibility, personal growth, direction and even accountability. Often times the avoidance of confrontation is rooted in fear. The fear of rejection or perhaps an emotional explosion on behalf of the confronted party is enough to shut down any means of constructive communication and interaction. As previously mentioned, confrontation was less than a fruitful endeavor in my home as a child.

For many reading this book and drawing from the real life experiences of those who have collaborated to author on the topic of endurance, I want to walk you through both the good and the challenging times I have spent on both sides of confrontation. I have had the benefit of confrontational reproof and been used in the initiation of confrontation. Both have been equally humbling, have borne fruit in repentance, and lead to culmination of obedience. It is not normal for anyone to awaken a day and be thrilled about being confronted or perhaps being the person to initiate confrontation. However, there are only three reasons any confrontation should take place.

I like to refer to them as *the three R's of confrontation.* The long term goal of any confrontation should exult in *restoration, reconciliation and righteousness.* If there are any other potential outcomes to confrontation, they are most likely rooted in fleshly pursuits and often times fruitless progress.

This author would like to walk you through two divergent scenarios that personify the need for endurance in confrontation as it relates to both the confronted and the confronter. I am thankful to have experienced both forms of confrontation and have learned invaluable life lessons from both sides of confrontation.

First, let's go all the way back to my early 20's where I was a young man struggling with issues of self-worth and personal identity. After several months of struggle, I found myself being invited to play in a day long softball tournament by a fellow co-worker with a group of men from his church. I was invited to attend church with him the following day. I remember distinctly the sermon from John 3 and the story of Nicodemus being preached that day. This story helped me to realize in a fresh new way how, in the midst of struggle and pain, an *intellectual relationship with Jesus* is not the place to find hope for my immediate circumstances much less my future. I too, had vacillated over the years drifting in and out of bouts of depression and great angst. After several weeks of contemplation and reflection, I found myself re-dedicating my life to Christ and desiring a discipling relationship with a man who exuded the love and mercy of the Lord. It was more than evident that Tom was a man who loved God in his role as pastor of the College and Career Ministry at the church. He was one who loved the Word of the Lord and equally loved the Lord of the Word. His ministry was well rooted in God's Word and Tom served a tremendous example of lifestyle evangelism and a solid disciple maker.

After sitting under such a man of God and being nurtured as a new disciple, Tom helped me learn to study the Word and grow in my understanding of Scripture. He used to amaze me with his ability to recite large passages of the Word and was more than proficient with the many addresses of passages and their application to everyday living. One of the things I most appreciated about Tom was his contagious desire to learn and teach the Word of God to young men and women seeking to honor and serve the Lord wherever they were called. He was the first to teach me the *"bloom where you are planted"* method of the Christian walk. It was through Tom's challenge to me as a young man that one should never attempt to seek out seminary training for vocational ministry, but to go to seminary because God has called you there.

That calling should be affirmed by those who have invested into one's mentorship and those members of the body of Christ who were benefited through personal ministry. That particular challenge has stood with me over the years as I have been blessed to with similar opportunities to reproduce other young disciples to learn and love the Word as well as its application.

Fast forward a couple of years and picture in your mind's eye a conversation regarding formal training to be equipped for vocational ministry. It was at this point in my growing faith that I was confronted with the issue of personal debt and lacking the freedom to be obedient to a ministry calling if the Lord would so choose to call me. I was living in disobedience to the principle of Scripture that addresses one's being in debt as a slave to a lender. It became obvious over time that I was on the receiving end of personal confrontation to develop a game plan that would free me from the bondage of debt and to walk in the freedom of being in a position to respond in obedience to the Lord's call to ministry should He choose to do so. This is where the true intensity of a battle for righteousness became a challenge for me.

It was a short time later through an intentional plan to become unshackled to my current debt that a game plan was put in place. I committed to whatever was necessary to change and live in obedience before God and my fellow church family. Within a one month process, I had sought out gainful employment to surrender as a debtor. I was fortunate to find three full time jobs as part of my personal plan to financial freedom. I spent the next two years working 120 hours a week and with the Lord's help and the body of Christ's support was able to extinguish over $100,000.00 in personal debt. It was through this humbling experience that the

Lord actually broke me as a young man. About 3 months into this grueling schedule, I had a vehicle repossession which forced me to ride a bicycle to and from work for the remainder of that time as my only means of transportation. It would be worth noting here that this was a very challenging time in my young adult life and I remember vividly a time where I broke down on the side of the road in repentance and tears crying out to God, *"How did I get to this place?"*

This life experience took place in the suburbs of Chicago, Illinois and as mentioned before, it was not without its struggles and pain. There were days where rain or shine, cold or intense heat, sleet, snow, beautiful days and extremely challenging weather conditions helped refine my personal fortitude to live out my redemptive potential in overcoming such an insurmountable circumstance that resulted from poor financial choices. It truly was my own personal trial where I learned obedience through the things that I suffered and grew tremendously in the Lord. I was on the receiving end of being confronted but with the help, love and commitment of my Pastor wanting me to demonstrate righteousness in daily living. I was able to experience financial freedom for the first time in my life at 28 years old. To this day, I look back and reflect on the many life lessons I carry with me and try to pass on to others and would not trade the fire for any form of comfort, as it has helped shape and mold me to the man I am today!

The alternative to being the recipient of confrontation is to perhaps be the one called to confront. Remember, if you will, the only reason for any confrontation to take place is when it is necessary to bring about *restoration, reconciliation and righteousness.* Please understand not every person is hard wired to feel comfortable being a confronter. It requires endurance because the party that initiates confrontation must be committed to seeing it through to completion.

It was only a couple of years ago that I was contacted by a dear brother in Christ to inquire if I would be willing to prayerfully consider mediating a church conflict issue in his church. We shared the context of men's ministry as a connection point and, after several days of prayer, it was more than evident that I was being led to step into the situation that needed to be addressed for the purpose of bringing reconciliation to a long term fracture in church relationships. Initially, it was necessary to meet those individuals between whom the relational chasm resided. This local body of believers was struggling from an unresolved long term conflict and was beginning to take its toll on the entire congregation. With the Lord's guidance, help and timing the mediation commenced and we were off and running. My friend and I scheduled a necessary meeting where we interviewed and listened to both parties individually to ascertain the root of the unresolved conflict. It was more than evident the pain and the hurt that had taken its toll over a body where raw emotions had been repressed and hidden as a result of what appeared to be maligning behavior. The importance of hearing both sides was amazing to learn from each perspective of the details and conclude that the details were consistent from each contributing party. However, what struck me as fascinating was that the interpretation of the details presented a vast difference. The perspectives of the conflict were as different as night and day. After taking time to pray over the content of the interviews and crying out for wisdom (James 1:2-6), it became apparent where the root cause of the original conflict resided. It resided in the unwillingness to address the root cause of the conflict, much less acknowledge it. It ultimately came down to the disobedience to the principle found in Scripture where Paul's instructs the Ephesian believers (Ephesians 4:26-27) to not allow the sun to go down on anger (perhaps unresolved conflict) thus giving the enemy an opportunity (stronghold, foothold). This unresolved conflict had spanned over a five year period without resolution.

It was a step in the right direction to determine which party felt maligned and perhaps had their character called into question over what was determined to be non-substantial accusations and non-validated facts. So imagine, if you will, allowing the sun to go down, day by day, over a period of five years without resolving conflict. This circumstance would not provide for a single opportunity for division and unrest, but perhaps a welcome mat to achieving long term residence for the enemy. Days turned into months that turned into years allowing pain to remain repressed and unaddressed and overflowing into bitterness, resentment, evil suspicions etc. Imagine, if you will, how you would have felt having your name tarnished in your small community without exoneration for such a period of time.

The role of mediation served as the opportunity to shine the light on the root issues of unforgiveness, buried bitterness, unrepentant hearts and long-term pain caused from personal pride. It was apparent from the initial meeting that one viable outcome could result in true reconciliation and restoration among this body of believers or perhaps continued dysfunction and broken relationships from within. The true challenge set before us was to determine the willingness on behalf of the factious parties to reconcile with one another. It also required that leadership be brought into this unfortunate turn of events for the purpose of providing accountability and a process from which to evaluate progress and necessary next-step solutions in moving forward to an amicable resolution.

It would be worth noting here that it was imperative to handle all information received with open hearts and open minds so as to ascertain the veracity of claims and present viable options for personal assignments that would speak life into what appeared to be a dying circumstance. We began with regular weekly *meetings* among those in conflict, regular weekly *assignments* among those in conflict, weekly *debriefings* among leadership and monthly *progress* presented to denominational overseers. This process also called for continual intercessory prayer on my behalf and those leaders seeking a positive outcome. It would be sufficient to understand that the greatest challenge was established by the enemy whose sole purpose is to steal, kill and destroy (John 10:10). Our role as leaders in such circumstances was to establish a foundation built on truth and provide an environment that allowed for opportunities to learn through self-discovery. Each person agreed to accountability and to remain faithful to completing assignments in a timely manner for evaluation and progress. There was much energy and effort put forth to allow each assignment to build on previous assignments thus indicating personal growth and progress.

Leaders were challenged to better understand the necessity of accountability among themselves and those they were entrusted to serve. They were stretched through personal assignments as well that helped them identify areas of strength in leadership. Equally so, many learned areas of weakness that included the challenge to confront situations for the purpose of preserving truth rather than maintaining the status quo of perceived harmony and unity. We thoroughly examined the biblical qualifications of their office based on character qualities and discussed by Paul in 1 Thessalonians 1:5-9 and 1 Timothy 3:1-7. These exercises allowed the opportunity for personal reflection and assessment of each leader's role in their church. There were some who came to the realization that they were perhaps not qualified or serving without understanding the full scope of responsibilities that accompanied their role in leadership. It was a very healthy step in assessing the overall health of their church flowing from leadership down to regularly attending members, and even visitors. Individual assessments and understanding created an atmosphere with sober evaluation and consideration of one another.

This opportunity to serve an active mediator for unresolved conflict with a congregation was one of the most challenging experiences I have had as a follower of Christ. It was fraught with intercessory prayer, dependence, discernment, affirmation and confirmation that the end goal must always be to preserve truth and maintain righteousness within the body of Christ. It is the understood goal of every believer to live at peace with one another, so long as it is up to us (Romans 12:18). The overall process took some 18 months to walk through with many shed tears, difficult confrontations and personal evaluation. After all that time, the results of many finished assignments, regular interaction and much instruction were turned over to the evaluation of the denomination. The denominational leaders assessed our experience with a request for the pastor to resign. It would be worth noting that this request for resignation resulted from an unwillingness to be reconciled and remaining unwilling to be accountable as a shepherd over his flock. Resignation was certainly never the goal in addressing the mediated conflict from the beginning. It was an unfortunate result, however, the church was assigned an interim pastor who has stepped into less than an ideal circumstance and led the body back to wholeness and health.

In closing, please note that the three steps to any confrontation must be to maintain *restoration, reconciliation and righteousness* as long-term goals. That goes for any confrontation, whether we are the recipients or the initiators of such a confrontation. Only through perseverance and a commitment to *GO THE DISTANCE* with confrontation can we maintain our integrity and grow in Christ-likeness in the process. For those who find this approach less than conventional, please assess your heart and motive before initiating confrontation. Perhaps, seek out some further guidance from leadership you serve under or feel free to contact me for follow-up questions that remain from reading this brief account of *Endurance* and *Going the Distance* inside the paradigm of confrontation.

STRATEGIES FOR BUILDING YOUR ENDURANCE

1. Are you a person that is comfortable with confrontation?

_____

_____

_____

2. What fears or anxieties must you overcome before you can step into confrontation in a healthy manner?

_____

_____

_____

_____

3. Have you ever found yourself on the receiving end of necessary confrontation? If so, what was the outcome in your personal growth?

_____

_____

_____

_____

4. What are the benefits you have received from being confronted by others?

_____

_____

_____

_____

5. Have you been called upon to confront a situation you know needs confronting and refused to step out in faith to do so? If so, how will you respond after reading this chapter?

_____

_____

_____

_____

6. How can your understanding of this concept of enduring confrontation better prepare you in the future in building healthy relationships?

_____

_____

_____

_____

7. Did this chapter help you realize that confrontation is not difficult so long as you keep the end goal in mind?

_____

_____

_____

_____

ABOUT TERRY WOOD

 Terry is a husband, father, son, brother, friend and most importantly a Man Following Christ. His life passion is to reproduce reproducers for the Kingdom. He serves as a life coach, speaker, author, businessman and entrepreneur.

His pursuit of reproduction has been built on the intentional principles gained from 30 years of self-employment as a contractor and being immersed in College and Young Adult ministry for 26+ years as a layperson. He currently serves as a team leader in an Adult Bible Fellowship at his church. His passion is to see lives transformed through the application of biblical principles in marketplace environments and daily living.

Terry is a family man devoted to creatively releasing the reproduction of healthy life disciplines, which will develop servant leaders who fully engage the Lord as ambassadors, through acts of love and devotion to God and others. He resides in northern Indiana where he is active in raising his two sons, Zachary 13, and Jacob 9, along side of his wife Becky of 17 years. His involvement in local men's ministry provides opportunities to hire and mentor young men while teaching them a trade to become self-sufficient entrepreneurs.

He established Break the Yoke Ministries to come along side of men needing direction and input to break the cycle of addictive lifestyle behaviors patterns and/or incarceration. His business allows him to assist others toward personal freedom and balance in life.

Contact Terry:
- Facebook: www.Facebook.com/Battle-Ready-Warrior-552634461573562
- Email: BattleReadyWarrior@gmail.com

JOURNEY TO THE SUMMIT: REDEFINED

By Tricia Andreassen

JOURNEY TO THE SUMMIT: REDEFINED

Why is it that can we feel so *unstoppable* in our mission in one moment and in the next moment we can feel like we are floundering, not able to accomplish our mission at all? The answer to this question appears to me when I have experienced a significant uphill climb to the top of the hill intentionally to see the big picture before me.

A scene comes to my mind from a day last year in which my husband Kurt and I jumped in the car to have a day together in the mountains. You see, we knew our mission: A. Get up early and enjoy the day together; B. See where the map takes us. I love days like this because we know that just being together with no other agenda will bring an exceptionally wonderful day. We also know that no matter where the map takes us our mission is so clear that we will find an incredible experience. As usual, we didn't know what exact destination we would reach, but we were certain it would be a wonderful day.

And, sure enough, it was. Like many of our excursions, we allowed for intuition to guide our drive. After walking in the little town of West Jefferson, NC, we continued on a country road that zigzagged alongside the flow of a rocky creek. It was a beautiful experience. We stopped along the way to admire the little cascades and fluttering butterflies that would pond on the rocks by the water's edge.

Throughout the day, we stayed focused on our mission of exploring and enjoying each other's company. As our journey unfolded, we landed on a country road that had a turn off onto a gravel road that you could tell would lead straight up the mountain. At first, we wondered if that road was open to the public, but we soon saw a roadside historical description of the place the gravel road would take us.

The sign for Whitetop Mountain indicated that, at the top of the mountain, folk music festivals were held in the 1930's. With music being my first love, I looked at Kurt and said, *"Well, how can we not go to the top of the mountain?!"* Our Yukon XL has always been a tool of wonderful blessing for exploration, so we had no worries about going up what felt like a nearly vertical incline to see where it led. Well, yes, I did have some worries. Who am I kidding? I was blessed to be on the Yukon's passenger side hugging the mountain, so close that I could touch the leaves on the tree. I was equally grateful that I was not the driver at the moment of the *"straight down over the mountain 'we could tumble' view."* In this reflection, my awareness grows of just how important it is to have someone alongside you when you climb a mountain. I love that Jesus is always with us to navigate in these moments, if we allow Him.

"Many peoples will come and say, 'Come, let us go up to the mountain of the LORD, to the temple of the God of Jacob. He will teach us His ways, so that we may walk in His paths.' The law will go out from Zion, the word of the LORD from Jerusalem."
Isaiah 2:3

As we reached the mountaintop, we were met with a view that gave us sight as far as the eye could see. The clouds decorated areas of the mountaintops in the distance. It was evident that we were at a summit higher than anything relatively close to our location. We later found out it was the second highest peak in the state of Virginia.

WOW! Isn't it amazing that when we set our sights with clear intention on an enjoyable experience that a mountaintop experience can be ours? The intention of having a wonderful, loving and memory-filled day was definitely being realized while on this mountain. What will forever stay in my mind was the view that was so vast and magnificent there. I was not prevented from seeing everything that was or could be before me. I was able to see mountain after mountain after mountain. The entire landscape of what God had created and what He *was still creating* became clearly shown to me.

"How beautiful on the mountains are the feet of those who bring good news, who proclaim peace, who bring good tidings, who proclaim salvation, who say to Zion, 'Your God reigns!'"
Isaiah 52:7

That is why I posed this question about why and how we get stuck and overwhelmed, once we get a taste of what can be. You see, just like gaining an unobstructed view of something so majestic from a mountain top, I experienced a *mountaintop filled to overflowing with insight* when meeting with Thelma Wells. Thelma is a wise woman who has gone through many mountain top experiences. She has been a leader in many landscapes as an Author alongside some of the greats like John Maxwell and as a Messenger willing to go the global distance, sharing the gospel through multi-media including television and preaching to filled stadiums of 20 thousand people and more.

As God would have it, my personal mission led me into a *"no doubt about it"* mountaintop experience in Thelma's home. There I was sitting in my PJ's sharing the calling God has put on my heart and collaborating with her on God's vision for her and for her ministry. This was so much of a mountain top experience that, when arriving back home, I was ambushed by the enemy's barrage from all sides.

What do I mean when I say *"from ALL SIDES"*?

...My son took a nasty fall on the stairs of our deck, bruised his entire arm and sprained his wrist causing him to miss school,

...A lady that I had admired, whose book I had endorsed (but not hired as her coach or publisher), and who had known of my character for 15 years, hurtfully attacked the very character on which I have built my whole life,

...A three-way conversation came out of nowhere that resurfaced brokenness and pain motivated by the self-protection behavior I have experienced in the family in which I was raised.

When I tell you *I felt like I went from the mountaintop to the valley within 24 hours* is no exaggeration. Even sharing this with you, I had no idea how difficult it would be to go from one extreme to the other. This experience of extremes has far too much potential to mess with our brains! Even with all the collaboration that took place with this wonderful woman of God and with her speaking God's Word into me to stay strong against the enemy and be fortified daily, I was still painfully challenged. In the rawness of this writing, I am *still walking through* the valley of this challenge. Yet, I *persist.*

I will *go the distance.*
I will *not quit.*
I will *endure.*
I will *keep my eyes upon Him.*

> *"I lift up my eyes to the hills— where does my Help come from? My Help comes from the LORD, the Maker of heaven and earth."*
> Psalm 121:1-2

For you see, I have seen the mountaintop and I am reminded of what I know God can do. I know that, if I do my part, *God will use my struggle to grow my strength.* He will use me to contribute to the fullness of the landscape much greater and grander than I am able to see from this vantage point.

It is not time for you or for me to quit. We know that God has placed His gifts inside us. We know the abundant love He has for us. We know that we can do all things through Christ as long as we allow Him to work freely in us. This is WHY WE MUST stay the course and GO THE DISTANCE! His Reward is greater than we can possibly imagine!

As I rest my muscles, my brain and my body from the upward climb to the mountaintop and from the bruising of the descent into the valley, I am reminded WHY this book is a critical resource for every single one of us. Know you are not alone. Consider every one of these Authors as your friend, your cheerleader and your partner. Know that within and beyond us is the ONE greater than all—the ONE Who loves you in the lowest depths of the valley and at the highest heights in your life. He will never leave you or forsake you. This is WHY, my friend, *HE HAS GONE THE DISTANCE FOR YOU so that you will GO THE DISTANCE WITH HIM!*

*"We remember before our God and Father your work produced by faith, your labor prompted by love and your **endurance** inspired by hope in our Lord Jesus Christ."*
1 Thessalonians 1:3

STRATEGIES FOR BUILDING YOUR ENDURANCE

1. Share a time in your life where you felt like you had a mountaintop experience. Perhaps it was achieving a goal, having a spiritual breakthrough or having victory over something in your life.

_____

_____

_____

_____

2. What did you learn about yourself in that journey?

_____

_____

_____

_____

3. When you go through a valley, what can you remind yourself to use as a tool to keep you moving forward? Hint: The insight will come from journaling through the questions above.

_____

_____

_____

_____

CPSIA information can be obtained
at www.ICGtesting.com
Printed in the USA
BVHW06s0738091018
529646BV00004B/7/P